THE TURNAROUND

THE TURNAROUND

WHAT SURVIVING BANKRUPTCY TAUGHT ME ABOUT ACHIEVING SUCCESS IN BUSINESS AND LIFE

GREGORY K. MCDONOUGH

LIONCREST
PUBLISHING

THE TURNAROUND

What Surviving Bankruptcy Taught Me About
Achieving Success in Business and Life

ISBN   978-1-61961-702-5 *Hardcover*

978-1-61961-703-2 *Paperback*

978-1-61961-704-9 *Ebook*

Thank you to my family for supporting me emotionally and financially through this journey and for keeping me motivated to train for my IRONMAN triathlons. I also want to thank my team for believing in the company through the highs and lows. The experiences shared in this book would not exist if not for all your hard work.

CONTENTS

———

FOREWORD

BY CAROLINE ADAMS MILLER

The first time I met Greg McDonough wasn't in an office or a conference room, and it wasn't at a meeting or a networking event. It was in a swimming pool, bleary-eyed at five o'clock in the morning.

He had signed up for the same swim program his then-girlfriend Monique and I had been attending—a competitive masters swim team class reserved for experienced swimmers. His reason for doing so was simple: He wanted to spend more time with Monique, the woman who would eventually become his wife, the mother of his two children, and the inspiration behind his pursuit of completing an IRONMAN triathlon.

Monique had already completed multiple IRONMAN triathlons and was actively training for future competitions, while I had been swimming competitively since my youth. Greg had his work cut out for him, but it quickly became apparent how highly he valued his commitment to the program. Greg slowly but surely shook the rust off his swimming muscles, which hadn't gotten much use since high school. He steadily improved his times. After a slow start, he eventually earned his way into the fast lane.

Three times per week with nothing at our disposal besides goggles, bathing suits, and sleep deprivation, we swam. We swam and swam and swam some more. As the weeks turned into months and the months turned into years, our friendship blossomed. Endless laps in the pool together gave way to dinners, barbecues, and other weekend gatherings. I watched Greg and Monique's relationship grow into marriage. I celebrated the joyous birth of their first daughter.

To show just how sleep deprived we all were at times, Greg initially told me during a swim session that they named their first daughter Simone. After swimming a few laps, he stopped me and said he'd forgotten his daughter's name in his exhaustion. Her *real* name was Sasha! He held on to the other name, though, using it on his next daughter when she arrived a few years later.

As the McDonough family grew and their professional lives expanded, Greg and Monique had to take a break from the masters team, continuing their training in the random pockets of time all new parents strive to find for their personal pursuits. As much as our commitments allowed, we still kept in touch over the next few years. Greg reached out to me in earnest when he made the decision to take on a larger role within EEI. He was already the company's CFO, but he wanted to pursue the role of CEO. He had a plan in place and a goal in mind, but he also recognized his goal required the development of additional skills to be achieved. Once again, he had to start slow and earn the right to "swim" in the fast lane.

Greg's demeanor is deceptive at times as his poker-faced exterior can hide his passion. But when he asked me to meet for lunch to discuss something important, I knew he was at a life-changing moment.

"I'm tired of thinking about what I want to do at EEI," he said as we faced each other over lunch. "I want you to help me turn those thoughts into action." He explained how he used his birthday as marker for annual growth and change, something I often see my best clients do to galvanize and motivate themselves to take decisive action.

Greg has the unique ability to bring together the right

pieces at the right time to keep moving toward his goals. He is willing to think outside the box and try new things. He sees the full picture before making a strategic decision—a rare and valuable attribute to have in life, and something that's served him well. He is not afraid of taking action.

Greg was always deeply passionate about the value EEI delivered to its clients, and he believed the company had a great team in place. Deep down, he knew he could make something positive out of the experience. He didn't see bankruptcy as a doomsday wave that would sink EEI's ship but as a rising tide that could help set EEI on a better path. Our coaching sessions became more focused when EEI decided to file for Chapter 11 bankruptcy in early 2012. As our discussions zeroed in on ways to achieve specific goals, one of Greg's defining character traits quickly emerged: grit.

Grit is the motivation to overcome all obstacles in your path to achieve long-term goals, and it can be cultivated throughout life. Research by psychologist Angela Duckworth has shown that half of human beings' ability to be gritty is innate. The other half is decided by what we choose to think about and act on every day. In my career as a performance coach working with people across the world to help them set and achieve goals, I've noticed three specific qualities that individuals with grit exhibit:

- *They ask themselves, "Why not?"* When faced with a potentially challenging situation, people with grit won't dwell on negativity and think, "Why me?" They'll embrace the situation with a "Why not?" and use it as a chance to grow.
- *They change the channel in their minds.* We've all found ourselves in situations where giving up felt like the easiest and most convenient way out. People with grit won't quit when faced with a challenge. Instead, they'll change their way of thinking and focus on finding a positive solution.
- *They create a team around them.* Every day, gritty individuals ask themselves, "Whom can I positively connect with today?" Life is not a path to be walked alone. The most successful people build a team around them for many reasons: comfort and support after setbacks, brainstorming ideas, and encouragement when facing new challenges, for example.

Greg exhibited all three of these qualities. Many business executives would have viewed bankruptcy as a defeat, but Greg saw it as an opportunity to make real change. Through our sessions, we were able to manage his stress levels through goal setting and positive psychology. This included identifying appropriate outside resources that could help him through the process, which led him to earn his certification in restructuring. Greg's list of accomplishments during our time together is impressive: He finished two IRONMAN triathlons, published a book, and launched a blog—all while successfully managing EEI out of bankruptcy.

Whether you are currently facing bankruptcy or are hoping to learn about bankruptcy's ins and outs in case you face it in the future, Greg's point of view will be an invaluable resource. He possesses a keen mindset for positive change and a willingness to try something new when old methods are ineffective. Learn from his journey. Follow in his footsteps. You'll eventually find yourself swimming the fast lane, too.

INTRODUCTION

YOU ARE NOT ALONE

———

I leaned back in my chair, let out a deep breath, and rubbed my eyes. They were heavy with fatigue, but there wasn't going to be any sleep that night.

I reached for the wineglass on the desk beside my computer. Empty. The first glass had turned into a second glass, and at that point in the wee hours of the night, I had lost count. A quick glance at the bottle I had opened earlier told me all I needed to know: It was empty.

My body ached from the day's triathlon training, but I had bigger concerns. I resisted opening another bottle and refocused on my work. I pulled up a fresh Google search page and went back to my research.

DESPERATE FOR ANSWERS

My company, Editorial Experts, Inc. (EEI), was being sued by our landlord. I was scared—scared of what the future held for me professionally but even more scared for the security of my wife and two-year-old daughter. It was early 2012, and EEI was headed down the path to bankruptcy. Why and how, I'll explain later. That night, as I had done many nights before, I scoured the Internet for answers to my questions:

What is bankruptcy? What does it actually mean? What is its impact on the company that declares it? What happens to the CEO, CFO, and all the other employees? What would the impact be on my professional future? What would it mean for my family and me? How would I get through it?

Those questions flooded my mind, repeating themselves over and over. Endless Google searches returned the same results: white papers written by law firms, research written by large turnaround firms, and pages and pages of dull legalese. It was beyond daunting to wrap my mind around all of it.

All I wanted—all I *needed*—was a simple guide that explained what bankruptcy was, what it meant, how to get through it, and what my alternative options were. What had it been like for other people who have gone through bankruptcy? There are certainly books out there on bankruptcy, but they are usually written more as process books. Where were the tales from the trenches?

As time went on and I became involved with Entrepreneurs' Organization, a global business network connecting entrepreneurs across more than fifty countries, it became clearer to me that I was not alone. Many entrepreneurial business owners don't even understand how to read a financial statement. When faced with bankruptcy, their backs are to the wall. They grind away just to make payroll week in and week out. They don't have the information they need, and they don't know the right practices to deal with their problems.

I can relate to the pain of finding yourself staring bleary-eyed at your computer late at night, wondering how to find help.

I've had many a sleepless night consumed by fears of bankruptcy. The unknown is scary, and I didn't know what awaited me back in 2012. But I made a conscious decision and found a way to face bankruptcy head-on by embracing it as a learning opportunity. When the dust settled, my company and I had both survived.

You can, too.

MY STORY

EEI was founded in 1972 as a document editing company operating in the Washington, DC, area. This was long before e-mail and other electronic methods of word processing, so EEI performed pickup, editing, and return deliveries of documents for other companies. That was EEI's primary service for the first few years until the company expanded to offer training services. After that, it added a staffing component, which allowed it to send editors, proofreaders, and desktop publishers to clients.

From there, EEI evolved along with technology, adding design and publication layout to its client services. Prior to when I joined in 2006 as its CFO, the company's previous thirty-five years had been relatively simple, involving mostly editing for clients. But as the economy became more complicated, so too did EEI's operations.

The first two things I did when I was hired as CFO were install a new accounting system and obtain a line of credit. From there, the company invested money in sales and marketing in an effort to grow the business. At the time I joined, the company was doing well to the tune of $11 million in revenue. Everything went swimmingly until about 2008 and 2009 when the economy suffered in the throes of the Great Recession. Our training division, one of the three main pillars of the company, went from bringing in $300,000 a month to $60,000 practically overnight.

There was significant overhead tied to that training business: 20,000 square feet of real estate space, IT leases, an IT staff, and instructors with curricula. It was a massive demand on cash for a business that had just had its revenue cut to the tune of 80 percent by the recession. From that point on, my role as CFO shifted from making sure debits and credits were right to planning *workouts*—or methods of restructuring debt so as to avoid bankruptcy—because we couldn't afford to pay the rent.

It became a difficult juggling act for me as CFO, trying to reduce IT expenses by letting people go while outsourcing some of the responsibility. It was the same story for our accounting department. From 2009 onward, I ran workouts with vendors and contractors and let employees go just to keep things flowing. By late 2011, EEI's landlord had grown weary of that arrangement and sued the company, believing EEI was going to be unable to pay what it owed.

This left precious few options on the table. We could either close the company for good, or we could file for bankruptcy and hope for the best. After considerable internal debate and multiple meetings with attorneys, the company's executives reached a collective decision: EEI was going to file for Chapter 11 bankruptcy.

LEARNING THE ROPES

As a result of the impending bankruptcy, I made the decision to learn as much as I could. I have undergraduate degrees in both finance and economics and a master's degree in finance, so I understood the numbers involved. What I didn't fully grasp was the process.

I found out about the Association of Insolvency & Restructuring Advisors (AIRA), a West Coast-based organization offering a certification program. In my application, I explained I was a CFO going into the Chapter 11 bankruptcy process and I wanted to learn as much as possible so that at the end of the journey, I could help other companies in the same situation. Three courses and one test later, I became a Certified Insolvency & Restructuring Advisor (CIRA).

One aspect of bankruptcy that is deeply important to me is the ethical side. Contractors, vendors, employees, and members of my family all felt financial pain during EEI's bankruptcy process. Those parties, excluding my family, had delivered services and earned revenue, yet they were not getting paid for it. Specifically, I recall a small business owner who lost $20,000 through no fault of their own: EEI set up their classes and accepted the payments for the class but spent the money on other past due bills. That has never sat well with me, and I've since been driven to help prevent that kind of situation from happening again.

BANKRUPTCY IS A TRIATHLON

You may be going through a tough time and are considering bankruptcy for your company. Maybe you're already going through the process right now. I know how difficult it can be. I know what it's like to toss and turn in bed, worrying about your financial future. I know what it's like to pore over pages and pages of mind-numbing Google results. I also know how important it is to have a positive outlet from bankruptcy. For me, my release was training for triathlons.

Sports were always a part of my life growing up, particularly soccer. But as scoring goals gave way to drinking beers in my college fraternity, my athletic career faded into obscurity. That changed after I met my wife, Monique, and adopted her passion for triathlon competitions. Triathlons were helpful for me not only for the physical benefits but also for how they helped me through the difficult period of EEI's bankruptcy. My morning workouts helped relieve stress, and when the endorphins kicked in,

I was able to think more clearly. No matter how hectic or pressing things got at the office, my training helped me maintain perspective throughout the day.

I continue my training and competing to this day. I find many of my best ideas come to me during workouts, and training also brings my family together as my wife and I include our daughters in double-stroller training runs around town. Balancing business, family, training, and annual races is a tricky but rewarding puzzle. In that regard, managing a business and approaching the bankruptcy process are really no different. There will always be great challenges to face, but overcoming obstacles produces rewards.

You don't have to train for IRONMAN triathlons, but it's important to find a healthy outlet to unwind from the stresses of managing a business. Bankruptcy can be a major source of negative energy. You need to turn that around.

In business, no one ever plans to lose a client or to miss payroll. Bumps in the road are going to come. Accepting them for what they are and being nimble enough to absorb them and adapt on the fly is what's important. When obstacles pop up—and they inevitably will—it's vital to keep moving forward. For me, it's similar to the challenges of triathlon training.

Keep in mind: Filing for bankruptcy isn't stopping—it's resetting.

WHOM THIS BOOK IS FOR

Bankruptcy is not the ultimate tool for everyone. It's important to remember it is just one option among many if your business is facing difficult financial obstacles or challenges. By the end of this book, you'll be able to recognize the classic warning signs of bankruptcy, which will give you the leverage to take a step back and reevaluate your business.

Each chapter includes a deeper examination of specific components of EEI's journey before, during, and after bankruptcy. These individual installments form an ongoing case study, highlighting what we did right, what we did wrong, why we did it, and how we did it.

After reading this book, you'll be able to understand:

· What bankruptcy entails.
· If and when to declare bankruptcy.
· How to take care of your employees.
· How to turn a company around.
· If necessary, when to dissolve a company.

If you're a business owner unsure of your company's financial position, this book is for you. If you're an aspiring entrepreneur looking for tips and advice on how to avoid common pitfalls, this book is for you. And if you're just looking to learn more about bankruptcy and what it means, this book is definitely for you.

Chapter One

BANKRUPTCY DOES NOT MEAN FAILURE

———

"Success is a journey, not a destination. The doing is often more important than the outcome."

—ARTHUR ASHE, PROFESSIONAL TENNIS PLAYER AND PRESIDENTIAL MEDAL OF FREEDOM RECIPIENT

Bankruptcy is a dirty word with ugly connotations in our society. People often think because they filed for bankruptcy, they're now branded with a permanent scarlet *B*. It's viewed as this unalterable failure that can never be overcome. That's all nonsense.

To understand what bankruptcy is, you must also understand what it isn't. Bankruptcy isn't a quick sprint from point A to point B. The entire process can take months, even years, but that doesn't mean it should be avoided out of fear. I embraced bankruptcy with the same mentality I did my first IRONMAN triathlon, understanding it required dedication, discipline, and preparation to complete the 2.4-mile swim, 112-mile bicycle ride, and 26.2-mile marathon in a single day.

Bankruptcy won't challenge you with cold, choppy waters and hilly terrain, but it will gauge your mettle through court dates, legal fees, and scrutiny of your business from outside parties. It's a different test of your endurance, but the mindset must be the same: Embrace the challenges by keeping your focus in the present and on the task at hand instead of the end result.

I wouldn't have been able to cross the finish line of an IRONMAN triathlon without months of daily training and proper nutrition. Likewise, I couldn't have successfully navigated a company through bankruptcy before first learning about the process. It will be a long, occasionally frustrating journey. But the bankruptcy path is one you can walk successfully if you focus on each step along the way.

The first item on your itinerary will be to learn what bankruptcy is and, just as importantly, what it isn't. There are a few major misconceptions about bankruptcy that I want to dispel right now.

MISCONCEPTIONS ABOUT BANKRUPTCY

- *Bankruptcy is a negative.* Here's the reality: We carry all experiences with us, positive and negative. That's part of being a human being. If you approach declaring bankruptcy as a negative, then it's going to be a negative experience for you. But if you approach it with an open mind, you'll find the outcome to be much more palatable.
- *Bankruptcy is a permanent blight.* Bankruptcy is *not* a permanent brand you'll be stuck wearing for the rest of your life, nor is it a professional death sentence. It's an opportunity for you to learn and can have a positive impact on your business. Treat it as such.
- *Bankruptcy is only for the big boys.* Bankruptcy is *not* just for major corporations. Small businesses and individuals file for bankruptcy all the time.
- *Bankruptcy is unavoidable.* Bankruptcy is not always the answer. This might seem counterintuitive, but it's something I will stress throughout the book. Many of the same outcomes from bankruptcy can be achieved simply by placing a greater emphasis on solving problems instead of putting out fires on a week-to-week basis in an attempt to avoid bankruptcy.
- *Bankruptcy is a personal black eye.* My business is important to me, but it isn't the only thing in my world. If your business fails, it doesn't mean *you* are a failure. Life is bigger than numbers on a page. When I need

to remind myself of that, I look to my older brother, Paul. He was born with brain damage that left him legally blind and with severe fine motor problems. Things that are daily basics for most of us are a challenge for him as a result, yet he has a love of life and infectious positivity. When it comes to bankruptcy, we need to remember to keep things in perspective. After all, black eyes heal.

DEFINING BANKRUPTCY

Bankruptcy is a formal legal process that allows for time to sort out everything that needs to be sorted out. That's purposely vague and broad, but that's what bankruptcy is in its simplest definition. The way that a legal process plays out can take different forms, of course.

Modern bankruptcy in the United States dates back to just before the start of the twentieth century. The Bankruptcy Act of 1898 marked the first time companies could be protected from creditors. That act has been amended and replaced multiple times since.

Again, forget the unfair stigma attached to the word *bankruptcy*. It's actually a useful tool to help companies restructure and reorganize different aspects of their business so as to remain viable. According to the American Bankruptcy Institute, 37,771 businesses filed for bankruptcy in 2016. That figure represents a 26 percent increase from 2015, but that type of fluctuation isn't abnormal. The economy, among other factors, has an impact on businesses. In recent years, we've seen many high-profile businesses successfully navigate through bankruptcy. General Motors, Kodak, American Airlines, and many others have gone through it and emerged for the better.

The physical process of filing for bankruptcy is quite simple. An attorney must file the paperwork on your company's behalf, but it's only a one- or two-page form that must be filled out at your local district court. It typically includes standard information such as your address, revenue, assets, and liabilities. As soon as the paperwork is filed, your case is open. That is what's known as a voluntary bankruptcy, which is the most common. On rare occasions, involuntary bankruptcy proceedings can be forced by creditors if they believe they are in danger of never getting repaid.

TYPES OF BANKRUPTCY

There are nine chapters of bankruptcy under the federal bankruptcy code, but the three most common are Chapter 11, Chapter 7, and Chapter 13. Those are also the only three that will be pertinent to you as a business owner.

CHAPTER 11: REORGANIZATION

Chapter 11 bankruptcy is a reorganization of finances in an effort to pay off debts owed to *creditors*—or parties who are owed money—while still keeping the business afloat. After the petition is filed in court, a *trustee* is appointed to work with the *debtor*—or the party declaring bankruptcy—to develop a repayment plan that covers the next handful of years.

During this process, the trustee will directly notify all creditors of the company's filing for Chapter 11 bankruptcy. Once the bankruptcy petition is filed with the court, it will be published in local newspapers. All bankruptcy filings are public information.

The court's notice to creditors will also include a deadline for creditors to file a proof of claim to recover what they are owed. All proofs of claim must be filed by a specific deadline, otherwise known as a *bar date*. Creditors' claims filed after the bar date are null and void. Once that deadline has occurred, the company starts working on the plan.

One key aspect of every bankruptcy plan is the *liquidation analysis*, which determines whether the company will eventually have more money to offer its creditors than it would in a liquidation fire sale. For instance, if a complete liquidation of your company would produce $10,000 for your creditors, but your plan showed you could pay them more than $10,000 after going through bankruptcy, the case will most likely continue under Chapter 11 protection. Alternatively, the case will be converted to Chapter 7 if the analysis shows that creditor would be better off in a liquidation.

Controlled Liquidation

The Chapter 11 bankruptcy process also allows for a controlled liquidation of assets. Through this process, the company, creditors, and judge agree that the best result for creditors would be to allow enough time to systematically liquidate assets, as opposed to a quick liquidation that is involved in a Chapter 7 bankruptcy.

Think of a high-end piece of art in which only one or two buyers are interested. If you're given more time to find those buyers, you'll get a much better price than if you simply took it down to the local flea market and sold it to the first person you saw.

363 Sale

A 363 sale is the process of going into Chapter 11 bankruptcy with the intention of selling the company as an entity, as opposed to selling off parts in a liquidation.

Equity Auction

After you've reorganized the company and the creditors have approved the plan, the final step in the Chapter 11 bankruptcy process is a new equity auction. In order to come out of bankruptcy as the same entity, you need to have new capital come into the business. This is done through an auction, which allows anyone interested in buying into the company to do just that.

CHAPTER 7: LIQUIDATION

Chapter 7 bankruptcy is a liquidation of all assets. This is the most common form of bankruptcy in the United States and can be petitioned by businesses and individuals alike. After your case is handed over to the court, a trustee is assigned to oversee the liquidation process, which essentially amounts to collecting and selling all of the assets.

As with Chapter 11, Chapter 7 includes a process in which creditors may file proofs of claim by a specific bar date. Creditors' claims filed after the bar date are null and void.

Once that deadline has occurred, the trustee has a clear understanding of all the pieces in place and begins to pay the creditors one by one. When the last dollar from the business's assets is spent, that's the end of the liquidation process.

CHAPTER 13: ADJUSTMENT OF DEBTS

Chapter 13 bankruptcy is almost identical to Chapter 11 bankruptcy, except specific limits are in place for the amount owed by the debtor. This form of bankruptcy is far less common than the two previous chapters.

CASE STUDY: BANKRUPTCY MINDSET

The first installment of this case study will explore the shift in my attitude toward bankruptcy from pessimistic to optimistic. Each chapter will include an additional installment that adds to the case study.

Circumstances

The economic recession of the late 2000s hit EEI particularly hard. The monthly revenue from its training business dropped roughly 80 percent unexpectedly and quickly, leaving the company scrambling to make ends meet. My focus as CFO shifted from managing the company's financial growth in an effort to foster further development to simply reaching workouts with the landlord to avoid being sued. By early 2012, that fear had become a reality. EEI could no longer afford to pay the rent. Fed up with the ongoing workouts, the landlord sued the company.

That was a major turning point for the organization. With no clear direction to follow, the decision was made to consult attorneys at a large-scale, global law firm. Their advice was less than ideal. They said EEI couldn't afford to go into bankruptcy because it would cost $100,000 up front, followed by an additional few hundred thousand dollars throughout the process. EEI, they explained, didn't have the cash flow to absorb that kind of financial commitment.

Options

Following the large law firm's response, EEI was left with three options:

- Attempt to smooth things over with the landlord and continue workouts.

- Shutter the business for good.

- Seek out a less expensive law firm for bankruptcy guidance.

A resolution on the landlord front was highly unlikely because the constant workouts were why he was suing in the first place. Closing the doors to the company was a possibility, but no one wanted to if it could be avoided. That left the third choice as the one to pursue.

EEI's CEO ultimately connected with a small, local law firm willing to take on our case. The smaller firm required about $50,000 over the first sixty days after filing, but they also made it clear I would need to take on the lion's share of the preparation for schedules. That strategy was far more manageable for EEI, so a deal was struck. EEI filed for bankruptcy shortly thereafter.

At that point, I personally had two options: approach bankruptcy with a negative, pessimistic mindset and look for a new job, or approach bankruptcy with a positive, optimistic mindset and fight for a company I believed in.

Decision

I can still vividly recall the wildly different atmospheres in the meetings with both law firms. When I sat in EEI's boardroom, listening to the attorney from the first firm, I felt hopeless. He was an older man with little sympathy toward the company's cause. He spoke matter-of-factly: EEI couldn't afford his firm's services. It was a bitter pill to swallow.

The meeting with the second firm was far more upbeat. The attorneys encouraged us to file for bankruptcy to put EEI under the built-in protection from further lawsuits and begin turning the company around. During the meeting, one of the attorneys turned to me and said, "You know, Greg, as the CFO of a business going through Chapter 11 bankruptcy, you're going to gain valuable experience few people in this world have. You're going to learn something most others haven't, and you'll be able to use that going forward in life."

Those words energized me in a profound way. I had made up my mind: I was going to embrace the bankruptcy path, dedicate myself to learning the ins and outs of the process, and make the best of the situation in front of me. I didn't want to go back to work for corporate America and fall into the nine-to-five rut again. I loved being part of a management team for a small business, and I felt like I had something to prove. I wanted to reach the finish line of the bankruptcy race.

Outcome

I started the information-gathering process where anyone would: the Internet. I found plenty of white papers written by large turnaround firms and plenty of guidance on personal bankruptcy, but nothing truly spoke to me as a small business executive. On a scale of one to ten, my knowledge of bankruptcy at that time was probably a two. Like anyone who follows the national news, I had heard about bankruptcies at companies such as American Airlines, Trump International, and Enron, but I didn't understand what bankruptcy actually entailed. Many of those major corporations seemed to use bankruptcy as an effective tool to reorganize, but to me, it seemed like an option reserved only for the big boys. I wanted to prove that theory wrong.

My mindset was simple but steadfast: What the hell? Let's do this. We have a great team and clients who will support us. Our fundamental business model is sound. We can afford the $50,000 to get started, so let's see what happens. I'll learn as we go along.

This approach to bankruptcy led me to become a CIRA who successfully guided EEI through the Chapter 11 process. Approaching bankruptcy with an optimistic mindset is the reason I was able to write this book. Had I bailed on EEI or gone into the bankruptcy proceedings with a pessimistic mindset, the outcome would have been much different.

Takeaways

Filing for Chapter 11 bankruptcy is not a means to an end. It's the start of a new journey, full of unique challenges and opportunities. There will be difficult days, weeks, and months ahead, but maintaining a positive attitude toward the process, and your business, will help you weather the ups and downs.

I wasn't always encouraged about the prospect of bankruptcy. In fact, I was downright discouraged by the idea until the boardroom meeting with EEI's attorneys. I left that meeting energized and excited about the opportunity to tackle bankruptcy, not frightened about the uncertainty of the future.

If you're feeling unsure about the bankruptcy process, that's normal and, quite frankly, to be expected. Stay positive. As you continue to read, open your mind to bankruptcy being a valuable tool—not a stigmatized failure.

HOW TO KEEP MOVING

Take a step back and ask yourself a few questions: Do you feel stuck? Do you feel the wheels spinning, but you're not getting anywhere? Is your company stuck in a rut and you don't know how to get out? If so, that's OK. You're not alone.

One of the reasons I fought so hard and so long to keep EEI afloat is because I didn't know anything different. I've always loved solving problems, and I'm very good at doing that. It was natural for me to keep trying, however futile the effort. When you get in the habit of constantly playing defense, putting out fires left and right, you eventually believe you have a problem-solving mindset that allows you to keep moving forward. But that tendency can have diminishing returns. It can even get in the way of the deep, fundamental, necessary change.

Before bankruptcy, this tendency made me reactive instead of proactive. I would walk into the office, check EEI's cash account balance, and figure out who I could pay and couldn't pay before waiting for the next problem to come along to solve. The next thing I knew, I was back in the same predicament two months later. That kind of situation is a classic indicator that bankruptcy could offer a solution.

What are your goals? What is the purpose of your company? Can you achieve them as your company is currently structured, or does something need to change? If change is necessary, bankruptcy might be the tool to give you time to make dramatic changes. Remember, bankruptcy doesn't mean failure.

THE BANKRUPTCY JOURNEY

People too often focus on the destination instead of the journey.

Whether it's training for a triathlon or dealing with bankruptcy, it's important to engage fully in the process. Your focus needs to be in the present rather than on the end result.

Ask yourself, "What did I learn today?"

By making small improvements every day, you naturally arrive at your destination in due time. When I crossed the finish line in my first IRONMAN triathlon, I vividly remember thinking about how to apply what I'd learned and accomplished to other areas of my life. Going through bankruptcy is no different. Two important things happened at the conclusion of EEI's bankruptcy process: the company had survived, and I'd gained valuable experience.

This book contains the knowledge of that experience. It's the guide you've been searching for—the one I wish had been available to me during my long, painful nights of Internet wandering.

QUESTIONS TO CONSIDER

These questions at the end of each chapter are intended to help you evaluate your company. There are no right or wrong answers; every company's situation is unique. By answering the questions honestly, you'll get a better sense of whether your company could utilize bankruptcy as an effective tool.

- Is your company's cash flow consistent and reliable?
- Is there enough available cash to cover the next payroll?
- Do you feel energized and have a strong belief in your business?

- Do you spend more time on revenue and growth tasks or on nonrevenue tasks?
- Are your financial statements timely and accurate, and are they used to help manage the business?

Chapter Two

A HARD LOOK AT THE NUMBERS

———

"Hope is not a strategy. Luck is not a factor. Fear is not an option."

—JAMES CAMERON, ACADEMY AWARD-
WINNING DIRECTOR AND FILMMAKER

The day EEI filed for bankruptcy felt similar to the day I signed up for my first IRONMAN triathlon. As the initial wave of stress from embracing new challenges melted away, both offered a combined sense of relief and anxiety. Those feelings quickly transitioned into an intense focus on the next steps.

The first sixty to ninety days after signing up for my first IRONMAN were focused on planning my training: when to run, when to swim, when to bike, for how long and how often. The sixty-to-ninety-day period after filing for bankruptcy was similarly heavy on planning but for a different kind of an endurance race. Instead of swims or runs of varying distances, I was completing tasks such as compiling a creditor list and notifying necessary parties we had filed for bankruptcy.

Completing an IRONMAN triathlon and going through bankruptcy are process-oriented procedures, but the first step in both is deciding to take the plunge. Mark Twain once said, "The secret to getting ahead is getting started. The secret to getting started is breaking your complex overwhelming tasks into small manageable tasks, and starting on the first one." Those are wise words to keep in mind as you move forward.

No one wakes up and decides haphazardly to complete an IRONMAN triathlon that same day with no previous training. It's impossible. Experienced competitors have died during these races. It requires months and months of training to prepare your mind and body for the rigors of a fourteen-plus-hour day of swimming, biking, and running. Respecting the race and the training process is paramount. That same mindset must be applied to bankruptcy: respect the process, make informed decisions along the way, and always move forward.

Before you can decide if bankruptcy is the right step for you and your business, you first have to determine whether you are right for bankruptcy. A top-to-bottom evaluation of all aspects of your business is crucial before going any further.

BANKRUPTCY RED FLAGS

Every business has different goals, different employees, and different challenges. There are, however, a handful of universal signals that indicate your business could benefit from declaring bankruptcy. Below are some common areas of concern for business owners to evaluate:

- **Time allocation:** How is your time and your employees' time being managed? Is it being used effectively and efficiently, or is there waste? If you're not getting the most out of people and their time, how can you adjust in a positive way? What needs to change?
- **Payroll:** Are you sweating making payroll, or do you have a cushion? How has that changed over the years? For instance, if you never worried about payroll two years ago, but it's now a weekly concern, that's a red flag.
- **Profitability:** Are you paying yourself? Is the company making any kind of profit, or are you breaking even at best? Profit should be sacred, but if you find yourself

considering what's left over each month after paying all expenses as "profit," that's a bad sign. If you're constantly in a break-even mentality, you'll be stuck in a perpetual cycle of catch-up. Profitability is an important area to focus on because it gives you the ability to weather the ups and downs—and trust me, there will be ups and downs.

- **Employee turnover:** Employees always have a sense of where the business currently stands and where it's going in the future. If you start losing key employees to new career opportunities, that can be a red flag. One or two employees leaving for other offers is fairly normal, but if it becomes a trend, that's an issue.
- **Taxes:** If you're missing payroll tax, that's a big red flag. Why? Well, for an entrepreneur, there's a personal liability associated with payroll taxes. You're the trustee of your payroll, so if the IRS doesn't receive those taxes, they'll come after the check signer, which is also you.

QUESTIONS TO ANSWER

What is your perception of bankruptcy? If you see it as a black eye, it's going to be difficult to manage your business through the process. It will become another project sitting on your to-do list that you don't want to deal with. Now is the time to challenge that mindset. Millions of people and companies not only survive bankruptcy but also thrive in its wake. Bankruptcy is a wonderful tool in the right situation.

Picture this hypothetical scenario: You're an upper-level employee, perhaps even an executive or CFO of a company struggling to pay back its creditors. You approach the owner of the company with an ideal proposal.

"We could cut all creditor issues by 90 percent," you say. "We can be free and clear to operate the business as we see fit for a year if we come up with a solution allowing us to pay creditors more than we would if we shut the doors. It's going to stop the headaches: the calls from creditors, the reactive approach to problems, the constant juggling act to break even. Would you be interested in that?"

What do you think their response would be? A resounding, "Yes, of course," right?

"Great," you answer back, "it's called bankruptcy." What would their response be then?

"Oh, well, wait...I don't know about that."

One of the biggest hurdles in the process is challenging initial assumptions about bankruptcy. Yes, bankruptcy will put new responsibilities on your plate. But at the end of the day, it becomes part of your daily and weekly routines. It's not nearly as cumbersome as most think.

Another reason people don't pursue bankruptcy is because they fear the time commitment. They don't think they can manage a company *and* a bankruptcy process simultaneously. In reality, this is another preconceived notion. Bankruptcy doesn't add that much to your day-to-day time commitment. It's important to challenge your own beliefs on what bankruptcy means to you, to your business, to your day-to-day operations, and to how your business is perceived in the community.

One technique I used is *time blocking*, which is an exercise in which you allocate specific amounts of time to each task you need to accomplish. You then spread these blocks out across your week, ensuring you accomplish all your important tasks. I've found this works particularly well for e-mail. I allocate two thirty-minute time slots each day to read and respond to e-mails. That way, I can be most productive while tackling the most important tasks.

It bears repeating that bankruptcy isn't always the answer for every business. However, learning about bankruptcy can open new avenues of thinking. When you deal with creditors, renegotiate a lease with a landlord, or plan for the future, you'll be better positioned to protect yourself.

Most importantly, you will have a more thorough understanding of your business.

There are a handful of questions every business owner must first answer:

- *How did I get here?* Your answers to the red-flag questions from earlier in this chapter will help provide guidance here. This is a literal question, not an emotional one. Don't ask yourself this in a negative, woe-is-me manner but in an analytical, evaluative manner. Evaluate your financials (where your money is spent) and your operations (where your time is spent). Figure out what has worked and what hasn't. It's led you and your company to this point. Look at this way: If you could start your business today with no debt, would you be doing the same things you are currently doing? If not, why?
- *What are my options?* The goal of this book isn't to convince you to file for bankruptcy. I want you to understand bankruptcy is a powerful process that can be used in the right situation, but the tools used during bankruptcy can be in your business arsenal. Understanding how bankruptcy works can give you the insight to better prepare for negotiations and other similar situations.
- *How do I move forward?* If you're spending today's profits on fixing the past, your business is not going

to grow. It's as simple as that. You need to invest in growth and invest in your people. You need to be positive and forward-looking. Most importantly, you need to trim the fat and figure out exactly what it is your business does best. Why does the phone ring? What does your company do that attracts clients? Figure that out, focus on it, and move forward.

- *What is my goal?* Many entrepreneurs are so excited to get started that they'll sign their name on any document in front of them just to keep the business moving forward. That's fine in the moment, but it sacrifices long-term stability. What are the goals for you, both personally and for your company? You can have one main goal to work toward, but a series of short-term, measurable goals along the way can help get you there.

- *What's the best/worst that can happen?* This is one of my personally recommended best practices, regardless of whether it applies to bankruptcy. As a business owner, it's crucial to project the best and worst potential outcomes for all situations. Know where your limits are, but also know your company's liquidation value and have a written game plan for the best- and worst-case scenarios. For example, one question I constantly kept an updated answer for was, *How could EEI maximize cash flow over the next ninety days?* If the goal was to maximize cash at all costs, I'd ask myself what changes could be made immediately.

ANALYZING YOUR ANSWERS

By answering the five previous questions, you'll gain a deeper understanding of your company's outlook. Is bankruptcy the right move for you? Maybe, maybe not, but you're getting closer to knowing that answer.

All too often, business owners develop a false sense of reality. Always remember: Getting by isn't getting ahead. Spending current profits on the past keeps the business afloat, but a closer look reveals deeper systemic issues that are preventing it from thriving. If a check comes in that enables payroll to be met in a given week, that's luck—and luck isn't a solution. Gathering information, keeping detailed records, and making more-informed decisions pave the way for solutions.

To conduct a quick analysis to gain a better sense of where your finances stand, compile a list of every party you sent money to in the last month. Make sure to include the invoice dates, due dates, and the actual payment dates. Once the list is compiled, take a close look at it. If you notice the majority of cash was spent on items over sixty days old, that's a formula for disaster. That's the rut EEI got stuck in, and it's a red flag.

MAINTAINING PERSPECTIVE

Taking a close, hard look at your company's financial situation and operational structure can be difficult. You might not like what you see, but it doesn't have to be permanent.

Sit back, take a deep breath, and repeat this phrase: The decision you ultimately make will not be fatal to you or your business. Your clients won't go away. Your employees won't all leave. Two years down the road, no one's going to remember that you filed for Chapter 11 bankruptcy. Think about it. Employees want to work and clients want service. If you've got something desirable to sell, clients are going to buy it.

It might be different if EEI sold aircraft carriers. Typically, no one wants to rely on a bankrupt business for that product, but EEI's clients and vendors didn't blink an eye. Many vendors raised their prices because our credit risk was higher, but they all got back on board.

The negative things you think could happen probably won't occur in the manner you expect, so keep a positive mindset. Don't tell yourself the sky is falling. Instead, tell yourself, "I'm going to file for bankruptcy, everyone's going to stay with me, I'm going to keep my clients, we're going to solve the past, reinvest in the future, and the company's going to grow." It's critical to take a step back and reflect. Think positively, set bigger goals, and keep chugging along.

CASE STUDY: DATA-GATHERING BLUEPRINT

This installment is not specifically tied to EEI's bankruptcy experience but instead offers a plan of action for gathering information and applying it to your own company's situation.

Circumstances

Remember the potential red flags we highlighted earlier in this chapter: time allocation, payroll, profitability, employee turnover, and taxes. If any of those sounded similar to your business, now is the time to review your practices with a closer evaluative eye.

As EEI's CFO, I was already intimately familiar with the company's financial numbers. But if you don't have a deeper understanding of your company's financial situation, there are different ratios that can help guide you.

Options

What are financial ratios, how are they used, and what are they used for? In the simplest of definitions, financial ratios are comparisons of different categories, and they are used to evaluate both the short-term and long-term outlook of a company.

There are dozens and dozens of different financial ratio formulas to choose from, but some are better suited to specifically gauge bankruptcy risk. These include the cash flow-to-debt ratio, debt/equity ratio, and the simple but effective current ratio.

Decision

The *cash flow-to-debt ratio* is calculated by dividing your company's operating cash flow by its total debt. This ratio is a type of debt coverage ratio that estimates how long it would take the company to pay its debts if it used all of its operating cash flow for repayment. The higher the ratio, the more likely a company can pay off its debts.

$$\text{Cash Flow-to-Debt Ratio} = \frac{\text{Operating Cash Flow}}{\text{Debt}}$$

The *debt/equity ratio* is calculated by dividing your company's total debt by its equity. This ratio measures the debt leverage of the company. It shows how much debt, as a comparison to equity, the company is using to finance its assets. A high debt-to-equity ratio is an indication of financial instability.

$$\text{Debt/Equity Ratio} = \frac{\text{Total Debt}}{\text{Total Equity}}$$

The *current ratio* is calculated by dividing your company's current assets by its current liabilities. This ratio illustrates the company's ability to pay its current debts with current assets. It is a measure of liquidity. A ratio under 1.0 indicates financial instability, as the company cannot pay its current obligations with current assets.

$$\text{Current Ratio} = \frac{\text{Current Assets}}{\text{Current Liabilities}}$$

In an effort to be thorough, it makes sense to run all three of these ratios through your CFO and financial executives. In fact, go beyond just these three formulas. Consult with a financial adviser or accountant if need be.

Outcome

Taking a closer look at your company's financial situation is a smart move regardless of whether bankruptcy is on the table. You should always have a grasp of what's happening financially.

Use the results from the different financial ratios as your fuel to start making changes on a deeper level. Poor financial ratios can reflect systemic and fundamental flaws within your business. Make a decision to change something.

Takeaways

Numbers never lie, or so the saying goes, but they can deceive you if the input is inaccurate. How do your financial ratios look? You likely had a strong idea of how they would compute, even before compiling anything.

Even if you're not the CFO of your business, I'm sure you have your finger on the pulse. If you read through the potential red flags and thought, "That sounds like my business," a hard look at the numbers will only confirm what you already expected.

WHO CAN HELP?

At this point, you've evaluated your company's financial and operational standing, so you have an understanding of what works and what needs to change. You know the questions to ask yourself and the red flags to look out for, but who can help you decide if bankruptcy is the correct path to follow?

This is a vulnerable time for business owners, and seeking help can feel like an admittance of failure. But as we'll explore deeper in the next chapter, that's simply false. Coaches and mentors are commonplace in other areas of society, including athletics, marriages, and academics, among many others. The business world shouldn't be any different.

QUESTIONS TO CONSIDER

These questions at the end of each chapter are intended to help you evaluate your company. There are no right or wrong answers; every company's situation is unique. By answering the questions honestly, you'll get a better sense of whether your company could utilize bankruptcy as an effective tool.

- Are your company's financial ratios stable?
- Is there enough cash in the bank to cover the next two payrolls?
- How steady has your flow of revenue been in the last three months?
- Has your company recently experienced increased employee turnover?
- Are you comfortable with your personal and total liabilities?

Chapter Three

WHO TO TRUST: ACCOUNTANTS, COACHES, AND COUNSEL

———

"It does not matter how slowly you go as long as you do not stop."

—CONFUCIUS, ANCIENT CHINESE PHILOSOPHER

We all need help sometimes. There's no shame in that. It's what makes us human. There's no way I could have crossed the finish line of an IRONMAN triathlon without the help of a coach, my gear, and the TrainingPeaks mobile training software app.

My coach and I use the app to track daily, weekly, and monthly training. Nine months before an IRONMAN triathlon, my weekly schedule might look something like this:

- Sunday: Long run
- Monday: Swim day
- Tuesday: Spin day
- Wednesday: Strength training/swim day
- Thursday: Short run
- Friday: Off day
- Saturday: Long bike ride

The training journey is about pace and a gradual buildup of endurance. The long runs and long rides increase by thirty minutes for three consecutive weeks, then taper back, then build for three weeks again, then taper back. Even six months before race day, my coach has my entire workout plan organized down to the day. It only changes if I suffer an injury or go on a vacation with the family, in which case, my coach realigns the plan. The value of having a coach to guide you through the process step by step can't be overstated.

Believe it or not, managing the ins and outs of bankruptcy is less meticulous than the daily training involved for an IRONMAN triathlon, but there are still similarities. IRONMAN training can mentally and physically drain you, and the bankruptcy process is no different. Some days will be tougher than others, but you do not have to go it alone.

DON'T DO THIS ALONE

There is no shortage of coaches in the athletic world. People hire coaches, fitness trainers, physical therapists, and chiropractors for their athletic lives. But when it comes to personal or business lives, there's more hesitation. Why is that? Hiring a coach is a leap of faith. It means you're not perfect, and that's a difficult thing for many people to admit, including strong-willed entrepreneurs.

Don't fall prey to this mindset. Simply having the ability to speak freely and get intelligent answers to questions will allow you to reprioritize your mindset. Embrace the addition of a coach as a positive. The lens through which you view a situation is important. For instance, I struggled with reading comprehension at an early age, and my parents hired a tutor to help me. I hated it. I saw it as punishment. They were forcing additional homework on me, keeping me from activities I enjoyed. I came into every session with the tutor with a negative mindset.

My daughter Sasha, on the other hand, embraced her reading tutor from day one. She looks forward to each session and greets the tutor with a smile. We had to push her to finish her reading exercises in the past, but now she constantly walks around with a book in her hand. There's been such a fundamental shift in her love and appreciation for learning to read that she gets visibly upset if the tutor calls in sick. "Daddy," she'll tell me, "it's my favorite part of the day." That's a completely different mindset than I had when I was her age. I believe it's because we framed her tutor as a coach, not as additional work.

Then again, I was always destined to prefer math, finances, and banking over reading. As a studying astrologer, my mother compiled my astrology chart when I was barely a year old, and the results were fascinating. Astrology charts are based on a million different factors—the time of your birth, the location, and the alignment of the stars, among many others. I don't fully understand it, but my mom certainly did when she created my chart. It said I was fated to love not only numbers but also choose a challenging path and forge it with a positive attitude.

To be clear, I'm not saying you need a personal astrology chart to solve entrepreneurial problems, but I firmly believe I went through the bankruptcy process with EEI because I was meant to do so. I believe in aura, and I believe positive things happen to positive people. Many people have asked me over the years, "Why are you doing this?" My response has always been the same: "Because this is what I'm supposed to be doing." Hope, gratitude, positivity—those are my biggest strengths.

I choose to be thankful for the people and things I have in my life. There will always be tough days, but I'm most appreciative during those times. I lean on others to make it easier, whether it's my wife, my triathlon coach, a life coach, an old business friend, or a new colleague in Entrepreneurs' Organization (EO).

WHERE TO LOOK FOR HELP

Accomplished volleyball coach and current USA Volleyball director of development John Kessel once said, "The pessimistic coach complains about the play. The optimistic coach expects it to change. The realistic coach adjusts what he can control." A great coach can make all the difference in the world, but how do you find one?

To find help as you weigh whether to pursue bankruptcy, there are two types of options at your disposal: professional and personal.

PROFESSIONAL OPTIONS

If you have a close friend who is either an attorney or an accountant, I'd recommend calling them first. By the nature of their professions, attorneys and accountants have had clients with businesses that failed and are thus great resources. Talk to them casually—off the clock if you have that kind of relationship with them—and ask about their clients' experiences.

A community like EO is also a valuable resource, providing important peer-to-peer connections with other business owners. If you asked ten business owners about bankruptcy, I'd guess at least five have considered it at some point and at least one has actually gone through it.

EO isn't the only avenue to connect with fellow business owners. It could be your local chamber of commerce, an alumni networking event, or even your sports club. It doesn't matter where, but find opportunities to ask some of your business-owner acquaintances if they've ever considered bankruptcy. If yes, why? If not, why? Also, ask them if they can recommend anyone else to speak with. The more information you soak up and the more experiences you digest, the better off you will be.

After that, I'd reach out to an investment banker. Most investment bankers have either bought or sold businesses going through bankruptcy. They'll be interested in meeting with you, as they make their living from helping companies pursue new opportunities. Sit down for an hour and have an open discussion about your situation. Similarly, merchant banks and turnaround firms for larger companies are also options.

As you will recall in chapter 2, EEI first consulted a large, international law firm that quoted the company a cost of $200,000—or approximately 10 percent of our annual revenue—over the first sixty days. That was too steep a price for EEI to absorb, but the company soon found a smaller firm to take our case for considerably less money. If you have to search for the right fit, don't be discouraged. There are plenty of smaller firms out there that are hungry, willing, and able to take on clients of a similar size and hunger level.

This is the time to note that bankruptcy isn't going to be cheap. There are legal fees, court fees, and trustee fees associated with every case. In larger cases, there are teams of accountants, as well as financial and turnaround advisers. The costs can add up rather quickly. That said, it won't be an exorbitant amount, otherwise no business would ever get through the process.

PERSONAL OPTIONS

Bankers, accountants, and attorneys are all valid options for seeking advice and collecting information, but so too are your friends. It could be a former colleague, golf partner, or a close college friend. Having a friend who knows your story, who will give you the time of day, and who can be a quick resource for you when you need them is critical.

Sometimes the line between professional and personal is blurred. For instance, some of my closest friends are also attorneys. Another friend is a lobbyist. A key part of being a business owner is developing a network of people who have confidence in you and respect you. When you're in need or have a difficult decision to make, you can reach out to them for a trusted opinion.

This is something we'll revisit in the next chapter, but it's worth mentioning now. You can't just be working all day, every day. You need to have an outlet from work, whether it's an organization like EO or your local chamber of commerce or your local triathlon club. EO helped me expand my network of business contacts in a meaningful way.

PREPARING YOURSELF

No one starts a business with the intention of going into bankruptcy, but everyone who starts a business should have a plan for when unexpected events affect it. Having a plan in place for every possibility, whether positive or negative, doesn't reflect a lack of confidence in yourself or your business. It reflects a preparedness for any situation that arises.

It's important to step back and take inventory of your business and life. What has the business accomplished so far? What are your goals for it moving forward? What are your goals in life? Answering these questions with a coach or mentor can help you keep a balance between the short term and long term.

In the short term, it's easy to go into the office on a daily basis and do what you're good at. But if that daily basis becomes a week-to-week and then a month-to-month basis, you've become stuck in a rut. If you're focused exclusively on the short term, you'll never be able to look at the bigger picture: What's the ultimate purpose of your business? What's your exit strategy? What's the long-term goal?

If you don't have that in mind, your business won't be able to reach its full potential. It will be subject to the waves of the economy and your clients. Not every potential outcome has to be negative. What if you reach a point where there's a new career opportunity and you want to move on from the business? Or maybe your husband or wife gets a job offer across the country. What happens to your business then? Things will always come up that catch you by surprise—that's just life. But the more possibilities you consider, the better prepared you'll be to avoid catastrophe.

When meeting with potential coaches, mentors, advisers, accountants, and other legal counsel, you must also be prepared. Be ready to answer questions about your business's operations and finances. Bring any and all pertinent data, including any recent bank statements, investment account statements, and any other specific financial analysis data.

Do your own research on potential legal representation. Don't be afraid to ask others for their opinions on another candidate. And, of course, listen to the advice you get from all parties in your meetings. Even if you don't end up working with someone or hiring them as a coach, they may still give you valuable information.

CASE STUDY: SEEKING HELP

The closer look at EEI continues with this next installment, which focuses on the importance of pursuing guidance and support from others.

Circumstances

When EEI entered bankruptcy, I held the role of CFO, but when the company emerged from bankruptcy, I was its owner and CEO. That was a unique transition for me that added additional layers to an already-challenging bankruptcy process, but I knew I was ready for it.

As the overseer of EEI's finances, I knew it was imperative the company shed the bad habits that led it to bankruptcy in the first place. If that didn't happen, the same problems were going to arise in the future.

I approached the board with a proposal that involved, among other things, my taking over as CEO. It also included restructuring the sales and marketing departments in an effort to get EEI headed in the right direction. The previous CEO became the chairman of the board, remained involved as a partner, and supported my vision to lead EEI through bankruptcy. The board signed off on it and made me CEO.

Options

While the move was great for me professionally, I knew I needed help to truly fulfill my own expectations. My background had been in finance, but I had to get away from bean counting to become a strong CEO. How could I do that effectively while simultaneously focusing on EEI's bankruptcy plan? The way I saw it, I had two options: go it alone or hire someone as a coach. That wasn't a difficult choice to make.

Coaching is critical. In recent years, I've had a triathlon coach, swim coach, and chiropractor each serve as support mechanisms for my triathlon hobby. In the business world, I had my friends and colleagues. Why wouldn't I look into adding a coach for my professional life?

The importance of having a support system to lean on—regardless of your profession or career interests—cannot be overstated, and it's a point I will revisit many times throughout this book. Whether it's an IRONMAN triathlon, bankruptcy, marriage, or any other challenge, don't try to be a hero. Michael Jordan is considered the greatest basketball player of all time, but he was surrounded by coaches his entire career. Every president of the United States has a cabinet full of advisers to turn to for guidance. I couldn't consider facing bankruptcy alone.

Decision

I was fortunate to have an ideal coaching candidate in mind from the start: Caroline Miller, a life and career coach, author, and prominent proponent of positive psychology. Monique and I had met Caroline, a former Division I swimmer at Harvard University, in the early 2000s during a masters swim class.

Monique was training for an upcoming IRONMAN triathlon in Lake Placid, but I wanted to pick up swimming again and started attending the class with her in the mornings. Caroline and I, both experienced swimmers, met in the fast lane and developed a friendship. Monique and I became close with Caroline and her husband, and we remained in touch even after leaving the class following Sasha's birth in 2009.

A few years later, I reached out to Caroline to discuss hiring her as a coach. It can be an interesting line to walk when you're hiring a friend, but after the two of us met for a long discussion over lunch, I was convinced it was the right fit. From that point on, we spoke every week, covering everything ranging from methods for talking to employees to setting goals. We stressed goal setting and time management.

Numbers and finances always came easy for me, but with Caroline's help, developing professional relationships also became one of my strengths. We worked together not only on challenges related to EEI but also on personal interests outside the office setting. For instance, Caroline and I came up with the idea for TriathlonParents.com, a website and resource dedicated to helping parents achieve their athletic goals. With Caroline's help, I was able to strike a healthy balance between EEI and my personal life.

Outcome

In a stroke of good fortune, Caroline's husband was a turn-around specialist, which is someone who helps companies facing bankruptcy or problems that could ultimately lead to bankruptcy. My work with Caroline, EEI's filing for bankruptcy, and my transition from CFO to CEO all happened in a short time, so I was looking for a way to learn as much as possible about successful methods for turning around businesses.

That's when Caroline directed me toward the Association of Insolvency & Restructuring Advisors (AIRA). I received my certification through AIRA, but the real value was in the program's lessons. I was able to experience the same specific bankruptcy restructuring education that an analyst at Goldman Sachs would have but was also able to implement those lessons in real time on a real business.

That knowledge and hands-on experience helped me during EEI's bankruptcy case and continues to help me now as I shift my career focus into consulting. Whether it's identifying creative solutions, fostering positive change, or just building some momentum, I have personal experience in each area. That's due in large part to AIRA's certification program, and the decision to pursue that certification came about after hiring Caroline as a coach.

Takeaways

Coaching and accountability are critical. This is not an area to overlook as your journey toward turning around your business begins. As an entrepreneur or small-business owner, it can sometimes feel like you're on an island. You can build a bridge off that island by hiring a coach, adviser, or consultant. You can also find solace in colleagues, friends, and family. Who to turn to, how much you can afford to pay them, and how often you two will talk are all personal and unique decisions you must make.

Hiring Caroline helped me stay focused and introduced me to new avenues of learning. When I meet anyone going into bankruptcy, the first things I suggest are purchasing the self-study materials from the bankruptcy associations and attending a few networking events to meet the industry players. These actions provide practical experience as well as an audience available for questions. They also allow you to avoid hiring a financial consultant or paying for an additional attorney. With the knowledge gained from the course work, I was able to construct twelve-week cash flow models, liquidation analysis, and other pertinent financial data that otherwise would have cost EEI the extra expense of hiring outside help.

None of that would have been possible without first reaching out to Caroline. Hiring her as my coach was a crucial decision and one that proved invaluable to guiding EEI through bankruptcy.

KEEP MOVING FORWARD

You may now have a deeper understanding of who to reach out to and what to look for as you weigh your decision to file for bankruptcy. This is a perfect time for a reminder: Don't be stubborn and don't remain isolated.

I could never have completed an IRONMAN triathlon without my support system. I need my wife, children, and parents for love and encouragement. I need my coach to guide me through my physical training. I need my chiropractor to keep my body feeling fresh. I'm not a superhero, and neither are you.

Don't try to carry the added weight of bankruptcy by yourself. Let someone else share the burden. Don't allow ego to get in the way of what is best for the business.

QUESTIONS TO CONSIDER

These questions at the end of each chapter are intended to help you evaluate your company. There are no right or wrong answers; every company's situation is unique. By answering the questions honestly, you'll get a better sense of whether your company could utilize bankruptcy as an effective tool.

- Do you have a firm grasp on your company's financial situation?
- Do you understand the cash flow of your business?
- Are your company's financial records updated and organized?
- Are you dedicating significant time and resources toward bankroll management?
- What percentage of revenue could you afford to pay potential advisers?

Chapter Four

PROTECT YOURSELF, PROTECT YOUR BUSINESS

"Success is getting what you want; happiness is wanting what you get."

—DALE CARNEGIE, AUTHOR OF HOW TO WIN FRIENDS
AND INFLUENCE PEOPLE AND SELF-HELP PIONEER

Taking the necessary steps to prepare for bankruptcy is as important as the bankruptcy process itself, if not more so. If you enter the proceedings prepared, you will successfully reach the finish line. If not, the chances of crossing the finish line are low, and you will most likely get injured along the way.

Being prepared for bankruptcy doesn't mean simply protecting yourself on the business side with tactics such as lowering the limits on your credit cards or making sure you pay yourself. What must come before that is protecting yourself on the personal side. How can you expect to successfully guide your business through bankruptcy if you're unhealthy, struggling to sleep, and unable to manage stress? You can't.

Navigating the bankruptcy process is like completing the stages of an IRONMAN triathlon, so that makes personal and financial protection like the pre-race training program that you adhere to. The methodology behind an IRONMAN training program is there for two reasons: to prepare you for race day and to prevent you from sustaining an injury. You might not tweak a hamstring or strain a muscle in court, but your wallet, reputation, and psyche can all take significant hits if you're unprepared.

Of course, getting a plan in place is only half the battle: you must follow it through to completion. That involves staying the course and hitting your daily milestones. Stay true to the plan and be mindful not to overexert yourself. That's how injuries occur in training. If the daily plan calls for a three-mile run, you have to resist the urge to tack on another mile or two, no matter how nice the weather is or how energized you feel in the moment. You're just playing with fire.

KNOW YOUR ROUTE

A regular part of my IRONMAN training over the years has involved long bike rides up and down Mount Weather, a hilly area just outside of Washington, DC, that includes a multibuilding complex controlled by the Department of Homeland Security. The Mount Weather Emergency Operations Center is used by the Federal Emergency Management Agency and is considered a relocation site in case of a national disaster. In other words, it's a heavily-guarded fortress, and it's a bit eerie. But the eighty-mile bike ride through the surrounding area is full of open country roads with challenging hills and climbs, and it provides a perfect training route.

There was one particular day while training for my first IRONMAN that taught me a valuable lesson about preparing for the unexpected. I had been invited by a few others to go for a ride around the Mount Weather area. It was the same distance I was accustomed to, so I figured I'd be able to handle it. Big mistake. Instead of the open country roads I was used to, the new route took me over cobblestone paths and alongside speeding cars and tractor trailers along Route 7.

The Snickersville country store I was used to stopping at on my usual route? It was nowhere to be found on the new one. When I finally reached the end of the eighty miles, my hands ached, my legs burned, and my body stung from dehydration, but I had learned a valuable lesson: Always protect yourself.

WHAT TO PROTECT

The term *protection* is broad and vague. What should you protect? How should you protect it? There are four main aspects of personal protection: family, career, reputation, and future.

- **Family:** No matter what was happening with EEI, I never exposed myself to the point where my children's college funds, our retirement plans, or our mortgage were in jeopardy. There were certain short-term deals I could have worked out to help EEI, but the added risk wasn't worth it.
- **Career:** Always have a number in mind. How much of yourself are you willing to expose? As an entrepreneur, it's easy to get in the habit of running up credit cards. In the moment, you're not worried about the next month—sometimes not even the next week. You can become so enamored with simply having a business at your fingertips that you won't notice if it starts to slip through your grasp. Set a limit for how much you're willing to personally invest and stick to it.
- **Reputation:** I put people first, almost always ahead of

myself. That's the way my parents are and that's the way I was raised. There were different times over the years I could have made decisions to benefit myself at the expense of others, but one of my core values is treating others with respect. I deeply valued providing as much stability as I could for everyone involved, whether it was EEI's employees, new vendors, or new contract partners. I was always up front and honest about EEI's financial situation and the future vision for the company. Those real conversations often highlighted the potential risks involved for the other party, which wasn't always easy. But sometimes doing the right thing isn't easy, and being transparent with others in business is the right thing to do.

· **Future:** Selflessness as a core value will pay dividends in the future. The same people you treated with kindness and respect will remember that. As a result, they'll be more willing to work with you again. If you worked with someone who genuinely tried to make the best of a difficult situation, you'd appreciate that, wouldn't you? Relationships are powerful in all walks of life but particularly so in the business community. The more connections you make over the years, the more likely you are to cross paths with the same people. Even if your business is struggling and potentially facing bankruptcy, your reputation as someone who does the right thing will help quell concerns.

HOW TO PROTECT YOURSELF

Your family, career, reputation, and future are the four pillars of personal protection, and there are specific steps you can take for each of them. Some of these preventative measures may require you to make changes in your personal life and business life. Change can create unknowns and that can be scary, but don't let that fear prevent you from making positive decisions.

If you're going to make a change for your business, make it on a deep level. Go for it. Don't just aim to break even because it's the path of least resistance. Changing things on a deeper, philosophical level can be painful, but pain is only temporary. Two or three months down the road, you won't have to worry about that issue anymore. If you continue to make decisions based on the paths of least resistance, you'll never be able to break out of the rut. Temporary fixes and Band-Aid solutions will continue to trump dramatic, positive change. That's what I struggled with for so many years. My first instinct was to solve problems as quickly as possible, so I'd work out the best deal in the moment. But three months later, I'd be back in the exact situation. It was beyond frustrating.

The whole purpose of running EEI was to generate wealth for my employees, for myself, and for my community through business transactions. I spent too much time focusing on simply keeping EEI afloat, rather than making it profitable. It lost its true purpose, becoming a burdensome project instead. The first step in changing that endless cycle is deciding you want to make a change.

Once you make the commitment to breaking the cycle, what specific steps can you take to better protect your business?

One step is to build savings into your future transactions. For example, if you can adopt the habit of taking 10 percent off the top of every payment you receive and placing it in a separate profit account, you will build up a sizable amount fairly quickly. Instead of your money being drawn from the bottom, you're proactively taking it right off the top. That's huge. Protect the bottom. Make it holy.

Let's say you forecast $1 million in revenue for the upcoming year. Right away, you know 10 percent ($100,000) is going in the profit account. That's not too shabby for a rainy day fund, but the challenge is staying disciplined enough not to dip into the fund. The next step is to figure out how to run your business with the remaining 90 percent of cash flow.

Another area to thoroughly evaluate is the breakdown of your finances. Specifically, what are your personal finances and business finances, personal expenses and business expenses? If they intersect, then where? Your business finances should always be kept separately from your personal finances, but as a business owner, there can be plenty of gray area. For instance, a golf trip to Arizona with friends who also happen to be clients is a personal trip, but it's also a business expense. You don't need to eliminate everything of that nature, but you absolutely need to evaluate everything you're spending money on. Trips, cars, memberships—everything. Can your business be more efficient with its spending? Could the money being spent on those half-personal, half-business expenses have a bigger impact if it was spent exclusively on business expenses? Maybe, maybe not. But it's something to consider.

If your business and personal bank accounts are one and the same, that's something to rectify as well. The more you can separate the two, the better. This can become a particular headache as you'll end up with unusable financial statements. When you're using the same account for your personal life and your business, there's little accountability of where the money went or what it was spent on. Keeping your personal accounts separate from your business also greatly reduces your financial exposure if times get tough.

I spent a lot of time with EEI living in fear of our issues. It's not easy to pick up the phone and call the IRS revenue officer who wants to collect thousands of dollars from you that you don't have. It's not easy to call the landlord you haven't paid recently. Trust me, I know the feeling. It's easier to put off those difficult calls, but the best plan of attack is getting out in front of everything. If your business is compromised, it's going to catch up to you one way or another, so pick up the phone and have those honest conversations. Let the other parties know what you're trying to do and why, even if you can't pay them at the moment. Overcommunicating tends to make the outcomes less painful: make them a partner in the situation instead of an adversary. Avoiding a potentially awkward conversation isn't going to make the problem disappear, so face it head-on and get the issue out in the open. You might be pleasantly surprised by the results.

There will be solutions available that you likely didn't consider. Perhaps the other party has a separate need that your business can assist them with. As someone who has spent years and years patching problems with deals, I know there's almost always a way to solve an issue. I say *almost* always because sometimes, no matter how proactive, flexible, and accommodating you are, others are going make irrational decisions that make your life more difficult.

DEALING WITH OTHERS

Not everyone you deal with will act rationally. This is a fact of life, and it certainly rings true in the business world. To use myself as an example, the company could not afford to both pay its employees and pay the bank. I reached out to our bank representative to inquire about a new payment plan or a potential settlement in full. The talks were productive and generally positive. I eventually proposed the idea of paying a lump sum to settle what was owed to them.

"I know it's not a ton of money," I told the banker, "but it's the best I can do, personally, and I think it's better than a liquidation." He was receptive to the idea, but it still had to be approved by a committee at the bank. The committee, it turned out, was not as receptive. They rejected the offer and responded with a counteroffer that the company couldn't afford. I didn't respond to it and instead focused on keeping things moving at EEI. But in late December 2016, I received a letter from the bank council stating that EEI's operating account was being swept. When a company is in default of a note, it's the bank's right to sweep the account, or offset any money still due with any cash remaining in the account.

I was frustrated because I was receptive to finding an alternative arrangement, whereas I felt the bank wasn't interested in working with me on a solution. I contacted them again and said, "Can you let me know if you're going to sweep the account again? If you do, I'm going to miss payroll. And if I miss payroll, my employees can't work, and we both want them working." In response, they instructed me to resume the original payment plan, which we couldn't do.

This is just one example of the other party not making the decision you might expect or hope them to. I try to avoid confrontation. One of my strengths is finding the right middle ground, but sometimes you can't avoid confronting an irrational person. When faced with such a situation, keep two things in mind: understand your own position, beliefs, and plan; and try to understand their point of view. To revisit the bank example from above, I can understand why the bank made that decision even though it was frustrating. The committee was following the bank's protocol, and it's far easier for the people involved to run through the process instead of getting emotionally involved and trying to work out a deal with me. The people in the bank were just doing what they were told.

If you find yourself in a similar situation, don't immediately default to standoffish and confrontational. Instead, listen to the other party and pick up as much information as you can. Try to be patient and understanding. Bankers and lawyers work in banks and law firms, respectively. They've probably never lived in your shoes as an entrepreneur and business owner. They have their own rules to follow and their own bosses to answer to. For them to get frustrated with you is pointless and, at the end of the day, a waste of time. Accept it as such and try to move forward in a positive, productive way. Life's too short to get bogged down in meaningless back-and-forths.

CASE STUDY: SETTING LIMITS

Deciding how much exposure you are willing to accept is the focus of the next installment of EEI's case study.

Circumstances

In late 2014, my wife had just left a company that went public. We had been invested in the company, so we ended up with some capital we could reinvest in EEI. After a lengthy discussion about the value of EEI, we decided to invest $100,000 to push through a slow patch. It proved to be the perfect boost the company needed at the right time. Fast forward another year to late 2015, and we found ourselves in the same situation after another macroeconomic change in our industry.

Options

The way I saw it, I had two choices: make another sizable investment of our own money, or work out new arrangements with the bank and landlord. Something had to give.

We knew the company's core business was solid and the team was strong, but at the end of the day, the return on the additional capital would be minimal as long as the company was burdened with debt.

Either EEI had to gain an influx in capital, or the payments to the bank and landlord had to be adjusted to align with the company's revenue run rate.

Decision

This was an easy choice for me to make. There was absolutely no way I was going to ask Monique again, as this time it would impact our kids' college savings. I limited the family commitment to that initial $70,000 and wasn't going to waver. Always set a limit to protect yourself and your family.

The decision to stop paying the bank and the landlord was

the only one at my disposal. I didn't make it lightly, but the only alternative was putting a sizable chunk of my own money into EEI. That simply wasn't going to work, as there was no capital available.

Outcome

I understood EEI's burden, post-bankruptcy, with the bank and the landlord, but I just wasn't willing to take on more risk just to make sure the bank got paid on time. It was a bold decision, but it was one that needed to be made to foster change.

As previously mentioned, things took a sharp turn when the bank ultimately decided to sweep EEI's account despite ongoing negotiations. The landlord was far more accommodating and allowed us to reach a new deal. These are the risks you take, but I have no regrets.

Takeaways

You have to draw the line somewhere. Why not draw it in front of yourself and your family? Putting your own money into your business is noble, but stop to ask yourself: Is it smart?

Is it worth risking your own safety and security for your business? Maybe. But is it worth risking the safety, security, and future of your partner or your children? That's something I could never recommend.

Set limits to how much exposure you are willing to take on. Most people get in the habit of setting three limits: the first "limit," which isn't taken seriously; the second limit, which is taken more seriously but still not viewed as deal-breaker; and the third limit, which is the absolute, drop-dead deal-breaker. That's a habit to avoid. Set your limits and stick to them. Remember, this is a risk-return analysis in which the risk is real and the return is based on hope.

IS BANKRUPTCY RIGHT FOR YOU?

If your business has certain circumstances you've tried your best to work out, don't wait until you're forced into bankruptcy like EEI. Why wait until you're sued by your landlord? Why wait until you've gotten into a combative relationship with your bank? Don't wait for those scenarios. If your business finds itself in a situation where it just can't catch up, bankruptcy can help get it on track.

If you're spending all of your profit to pay for things in the past and you're unable to reinvest in the future, bankruptcy is a viable option for you. Don't simply consider bankruptcy a tool to use to avoid being sued. Instead, view it as a tool to help turn your business around.

QUESTIONS TO CONSIDER

These questions at the end of each chapter are intended to help you evaluate your company. There are no right or wrong answers; every company's situation is unique. By answering the questions honestly, you'll get a better sense of whether your company could utilize bankruptcy as an effective tool.

- How much personal exposure would you have if your company closed today?
- How much, if at all, has that level of exposure changed over the last three months?

- Do you have key vendors/partners who would be interested in assuming parts of your business?
- Do you have a group of family members and/or friends to lean on for support?
- Are you worried about your company's long-term stability and viability?

Chapter Five

WHEN IT'S TIME TO DECLARE

———

"Move out of your comfort zone. You can only grow if you are willing to feel awkward and uncomfortable when you try something new."

—BRIAN TRACY, SELF-IMPROVEMENT
AUTHOR AND MOTIVATIONAL SPEAKER

Time slows to a crawl the night before an IRONMAN triathlon as the combination of excitement, anticipation, and nervousness makes sleep difficult. The ticking seconds become minutes, and those can become hours before your mind stops racing. Relaxation and meditation are your best friends at such a time, but it's common to have that nagging worry in the back of your mind.

Compared to the endless night on the eve of a race, the morning of an IRONMAN triathlon is a highly structured and organized whirlwind. Every hour leading up to the start of the race is broken down into fifteen-minute increments, with time allotted for food, proper hydration, bag checks, and even bathroom trips. Are my bags packed? Have I forgotten anything? Are my bicycle tires pumped up? Every question you can imagine—and many others you can't—will race through your head in the tense moments leading up to the start of the race.

It's human nature to worry about an important event in our lives, whether it's an important job interview, a crucial investor meeting, an IRONMAN triathlon, or filing for bankruptcy. I make sure to arrive at my race sites much earlier than needed, not only to soak in the palpable pre-race energy but also to avoid rushing. The last thing I need before starting a fourteen-plus-hour day of exertion is a rushed, stressed start. The pre-race nerves are inevitable, but it's in those moments I remember to trust my training.

DEVELOP YOUR TECHNIQUES

If you've been practicing a routine for something specific like a race, you'll be amazed at how instinctively your mind and body will repeat the movements. When I complete the swim stage and begin the transition out of my wetsuit into my bicycle jersey, I find myself surrounded by many of the other two thousand or so competitors, all stressed and stumbling toward their bikes in a big mess of humanity. Yet I, on the other hand, remain calm and relaxed, and move at a controlled pace because I understand I've prepared as best as I can.

I don't plan for a flat tire forty miles into the bicycle stage, for instance, but I'm prepared if it happens. Quitting the triathlon mid-race isn't an option, so I have to calmly fix the flat and keep moving forward. No one begins a business with the intention of declaring bankruptcy, but by taking the steps we've outlined so far, it's a path that can be successfully navigated.

If you've followed your training plan for the year leading up to the race, you will be ready for the rigors ahead. Declaring for bankruptcy is no different: Have a plan and execute it. Will there be moments that test you? Absolutely. Everyone who's ever gone through bankruptcy, completed an IRONMAN, or successfully completed another time-consuming and energy-draining task has thought, "I can't do this." If they say otherwise, they're lying. When that thought enters your mind, remember to trust your training, preparation, and most importantly, yourself.

You can do this by practicing and perfecting different

relaxation techniques. My parents introduced me to the concept of mind control and meditation as a child, but I didn't gain a true appreciation of it until my stress levels rose at EEI. Meditation is a deeply personal practice that means something different to everyone, but most gurus will tell you meditation must have a purpose. If you want to become a friendlier person in life, for instance, you would practice seeing yourself being friendlier during meditation. Your mindset controls how you feel. If you have a positive mindset, you'll feel positive; if you have a negative mindset, you'll feel negative. A simple recall technique to increase positive thinking is to focus on events you associate with happiness, such as a wedding, party, or other special occasion.

Along those same lines, developing a sleep methodology that works for you is crucial. Some people are blessed with the ability to fall asleep as soon as their head hits the pillow. I am not one of those people, so I had to formulate multiple techniques to help my stressed mind stop running at a thousand miles per hour each night. Some are simple, such as counting or listening to music, while others are more focused. I highly recommend a mobile app such as Headspace, which offers guided meditation and mindfulness exercises.

Some nights you'll fall asleep naturally without any effort, but during the nights full of tossing and turning, try this short routine: Take slow, deep breaths as you visualize your next day and what you hope to accomplish. After you have done that, focus on relaxing your feet. Next, relax your knees, and after that, your shoulders.

You will be in a drowsy sleep state before you know it, and then—*boom*—you'll be asleep. Keeping a refreshed and clear mind is absolutely necessary for successfully turning your business around, and the most effective way to ensure that is by getting consistent sleep. Only when you're rested and thinking clearly can you evaluate where your business stands, where it's going, and how bankruptcy can play a helpful role.

MAKING THE DECISION

One of humankind's most frustrating habits is to view tasks in front of them as daunting, occasionally unconquerable burdens. Break that habit. Running a business, declaring bankruptcy, completing an IRONMAN triathlon—these are all opportunities, not burdens. And, interestingly enough, what do we typically tell ourselves after finishing one of these big, insurmountable tasks? *That wasn't so bad.*

When I crossed the finish line of my first IRONMAN

triathlon in front of hundreds of spectators, emotion poured over me. My wife, children, and parents were all in attendance, and finishing such a physically and mentally draining event in their presence gave me an incredible sense of pride and accomplishment. The path to the finish line in bankruptcy is admittedly a longer, winding road, but the feeling of pride and accomplishment was equally satisfying. But how do you know if bankruptcy is the right path for you and your business? We've previously highlighted the red flags that all business owners and entrepreneurs should watch for, but this is the perfect time to revisit them.

ALLOCATION OF TIME

How and where are you spending your time? If you're spending much of your business life digging out of holes and trying to put out fires left and right, that's a real indicator a bigger change is necessary. Spending time trying to repair the past instead of growing and taking the business to new heights is a classic example of two steps forward, one step back.

This kind of tinkering works in the moment but at the expense of the future. I tinkered with EEI for years and years, accepting the least painful option at the time. But after a few months would pass, the same issue would arise and I'd be right back to square one.

I spent more time looking backward than I did forward. If you find yourself in the same situation, bankruptcy can help stop that cycle.

DRAMATIC CHANGE

If there's a major, often unexpected change to your business revenue, bankruptcy can help. For example, EEI took a massive hit in 2008 when the economy bottomed out. The company's revenue from its training business dropped from $300,000 a month to just $60,000.

If your business has gone through any kind of similar swing, use this as an opportunity to step back and evaluate your options. If the loss of revenue is too severe, bankruptcy might be your only option.

LANDLORDS, VENDORS, CLIENTS

Are you missing rent on a consistent basis? Are you unable to pay vendors and clients? If so, you almost certainly find yourself crafting corporate workout after corporate workout to stay above water. The purpose of business is to generate wealth for those involved by creating value for those the business serves.

These workouts can take many different forms, but the

two most common are payment plans and lump sum settlements. A payment plan is just what it sounds like. Let's say EEI owed the landlord $50,000 in past due rent. If the rent was $5,000 a month, we could ask the landlord to raise it to $6,000 a month for the next fifty months to make up the difference.

The other approach would be trying to get a full settlement, but that can be tricky with landlords. They have the leverage because your business is occupying their space, and relocating is a major headache. However, you can reclaim some of that leverage by understanding your options in a bankruptcy proceeding. Landlords deal with it all the time and certainly know how much it will cost them legally and their expected outcome. They most likely have rules and procedures when dealing with clients in bankruptcy, so they might not budge during a pre-bankruptcy negotiation.

EEI worked out settlements with many key vendors and clients, particularly from the training business. The lump sum settlement was the most effective. If EEI owed a vendor $25,000 but I could offer them $5,000 right then and there, many of them would accept the offer.

One tactic I learned recently but have not personally used is to send the creditor a check with "Payment in Full" on the front. Include a letter explaining the situation, asking for more time, and stating that you intend to pay them in full at some point in the future. State that the company can only afford to pay the amount included with the letter as a full payment for the debt. Inform the creditor the check is the best the company can do right now. Make it their choice to cash the check or not and mention that you plan to cancel the check within a short time. The source of this tactic experienced that most creditors will deposit the check and settle the account, as cash in hand seems more appealing than waiting.

I've always preferred lump sum settlements to payment plans because the settlements felt more final. Payment plans merely delay the inevitable. I much preferred sitting down with someone and having an honest conversation about what EEI could offer in the moment, rather than dragging it out. Most people, like me, just wanted their deal to reach a conclusion.

If you're noticing these three red flags, bankruptcy is a viable option that should be pursued as a tool to turn around your business.

PROTOCOL FOR EMPLOYEES

As the owner of your business, the decision to file for bankruptcy is an important one not only for yourself but for your employees as well. Their job with your company is their livelihood and primary source of income, so it's important to keep them updated on the company's future.

Smaller businesses like EEI have the advantage of being able to pull all of their employees together in one room for a conversation about bankruptcy. But that 2012 discussion in EEI's offices didn't come out of the blue. Employees generally have a sense about what's happening within their company, both positive and negative. When the economy swung in 2008, we communicated its impact on the training business to our employees. It was important to me to keep them in the loop along the way so that when EEI officially filed for bankruptcy, it didn't come as a shock.

In fact, shortly after the bankruptcy filing, we pulled everyone together and delivered a positive message: Nothing is wrong with our business. We emphasized that EEI was a strong business that had gone through the ups and downs of the economy and survived to that point but just had too much legacy debt on the books to continue to move forward. In order to relieve that debt, we explained, we were filing for Chapter 11 bankruptcy, which sounds dire but is actually an effective tool that countless businesses have used to their advantage.

Explain that Chapter 11 bankruptcy isn't a complete liquidation. They'll still have their jobs. Be open, honest, and empathetic. Listen to any questions and answer them as thoroughly as possible. It's unavoidable that some employees may leave the company for other opportunities, but typically, most will just roll with it.

WHAT HAPPENS?

The day your company files for bankruptcy is largely anticlimactic. As the business owner, you're not required to physically visit court for the filing process. That is handled by your attorney, either through e-filing or in person at the local clerk's office. The timing of the filing is noteworthy, though.

In EEI's case, the company was prohibited from using any cash for operations without the consent of the bank once the paperwork was filed. We held discussions with the bank about their cash collateral agreement, and whether they would allow us to use any cash we received from collecting account receivables to keep the business going. This is a critical conversation to have. Once you file for bankruptcy, you're not allowed to use the bank's collateral without their permission. That's why EEI filed on February 15, 2012—a Wednesday, the day after our payroll had been run. That gave us a two-week window to come up with an agreement with the bank. If you're able to file for bankruptcy in the same manner, it will buy you as much additional time as possible to square away things with the bank or other entity with security interest in the company assets. In other cases, companies have been able to raise money through debtor-in-possession (DIP) financing after filing for bankruptcy. The advantage to the DIP lender is they receive a priority over all other debts.

The first thirty to sixty days following filing for bankruptcy is full of paperwork, notices to creditors, and attorney dealings. It's not the time for self-pity or even reflection. You'll be too busy to sit and ponder things. Prioritizing your days and weeks will become a critical balancing act. Every bankruptcy case will have its own unique wrinkles exclusive to the company, but there are standard procedures that universally apply:

- **Trustee meeting:** Within a week of filing for bankruptcy, there will be a meeting scheduled with the court-appointed US trustee, your legal counsel, the landlord's attorney, and the bank's attorney. You should attend this meeting, but it will consist exclusively of discussions among the attorneys. It's essentially an hour-long meet-and-greet to get everyone up to speed.
- **Creditor meeting:** The next step is the 341 hearing, which comes three to five weeks after the bank-

ruptcy filing. This is typically the only meeting you're required to attend, but consult with your legal counsel for guidance specific to your case. At this meeting, the trustee can ask you and your counsel questions under oath about your business's information and finances. Creditors have previously been sent notice about your bankruptcy filing, so this meeting presents an opportunity for them to gain a better understanding of the parameters of the filing.

- **Monthly reporting:** While you're in bankruptcy, you need to report on a monthly basis to the court using a standardized form that includes your income statement, balance sheet, and cash flow statement. The form also includes money collected, money spent, and a cash flow forecast. All of that information is posted in a bankruptcy case docket and becomes publicly available information. This is all administrative in nature, but the main idea is to show the court you are keeping the business alive and have a plan for your creditors that's better than a complete liquidation of your company.

- **Determine classes:** This exercise will arise during the creation of your plan, but it's worth highlighting on its own. In bankruptcy cases, all creditors are divvied up into classes. For instance, the bank was in EEI's class A because they were the only creditor secured by assets of the business. Tax liabilities were class B.

Employees and their accrued vacation time were class C. Vendors where split up between class D and class E, depending of what type of service they offered the company. What is the purpose of this? Once your plan is submitted to the court, it is then sent out to each entity in the different classes for an approval vote. If all of the classes approve the plan, it moves forward. If one class approves it but the others vote no, the judge will determine whether the plan is fair. If all of the classes vote against it, the judge won't even consider the plan.

- **Turnaround plan:** Within twelve months of filing for bankruptcy, you have to submit a long-term plan to the court. The plan then gets distributed via mail to the creditors. This plan can be revised if other parties request it. For instance, after EEI submitted its plan, the bank took issue with a specific section, so we had to revise it. This plan can be continuously updated and revised, but each time something is amended or added, you have to file that with the court.

- **Get out of bankruptcy:** Once the plan is submitted and approved by your creditors, you and your legal counsel will attest to such in front of the judge. Once the judge approves everything, a date will be set for a new equity auction, if that was included in your plan. Over the next thirty days, bids will be collected. That is typically the last step of the bankruptcy process.

- **Stay out of bankruptcy:** Once you come out of bankruptcy, you're still required to report to the court on a quarterly basis. This consists of a standardized form detailing how much you paid and to whom according to the agreed-upon plan. In essence, it's a simple way to verify you've remained true to the terms of the plan. After a year—or four quarterly reports—your attorney can make a motion to the court stating you've complied with all of the requirements and asking for a conclusion to the required reports. If the court approves it, that's typically when the involvement of the attorneys and the judge comes to an end. You'll still be paying creditors as dictated in the plan, but you'll no longer be under scrutiny. For all intents and purposes, it's back to business as normal.

ADVANTAGES OF BANKRUPTCY

There are many favorable reasons to file for bankruptcy, but perhaps the most critical is that it allows you to handle all your legacy debt in one fell swoop while under protection. This can't be overstated. Instead of scrambling on a daily, weekly, and monthly basis to figure out what you can pay this vendor and that creditor, bankruptcy straightens all that out. It gets everyone on the same page with the same payment plan moving forward. All of that uneasiness about debts owed on past deals dissipates, and you're able to finally move the business forward.

Statutory contracts, also known as executory contracts, can also be broken during bankruptcy. This requires the trustee's approval, but it can be a major benefit to companies seeking to get out of lengthy and/or expensive leases. EEI had IT leases, computer leases, copiers—everything you'd expect a modern business to have. We were able to break most of those leases, which saved the company considerable amounts of money.

Another major advantage of bankruptcy is that it will inject new life into your business. By going through the bankruptcy process, you've evaluated your business from top to bottom and inevitably cleaned up some things on the books you weren't thrilled with. You've taken a close look at everything, from the allocation of your employees' time to your business and personal expenses. That's a valuable practice for any business, whether bankruptcy is on the table or not.

On a personal level, there's a sense of accomplishment for getting through bankruptcy, much like finishing an IRON-MAN triathlon. You've studied, planned, and trained, and you've seen your game plan through from start to finish. That's a feather in your cap, both personally and professionally. Like every other experience in life, bankruptcy is a chance to learn and grow. Successfully guiding a company through bankruptcy will earn you respect in the business world and help boost your reputation as an entrepreneur who embraces every avenue to help the company succeed.

CASE STUDY: TIMING OF FILING

EEI would have been better off had it filed for bankruptcy in 2009 as opposed to 2012. We'll explore why in this next case study installment.

Circumstances

In the first few years after I joined EEI, the company was bringing in $11 million in overall annual revenue. That allowed us to invest money in sales and marketing to continue growing the business. Everything was progressing swimmingly until the economy turned in 2009.

EEI's training business was hit the hardest. That branch went from bringing in $300,000 a month to $60,000 basically overnight. That loss of revenue was devastating enough, but considering the substantial overhead EEI had tied to the business, it exacerbated existing issues. We had 20,000 square feet of real estate space, IT leases, IT staff, and instructors with curriculums. It was a lot of demand for cash on a business that had just been cut by 80 percent. The majority of our training clients were association employees and government employees, so when the economy turned and the housing market imploded, there was a major decline in money spent on training.

Once that happened, my role as CFO shifted dramatically. I went from managing EEI's accounting team as well as its financing and growth to piecing together workout after workout because we suddenly couldn't afford to pay the rent.

As more and more people were laid off around the Washington, DC, area, unemployment continued to rise. That major shift in the economy was the biggest hit to EEI's training business, but it wasn't the only factor. In retrospect, EEI was behind the curve with virtual training programs. I still believe instructor-led training is the most efficient method of teaching, but EEI should have been offering more virtual or e-learning solutions allowing for more exposure at lower costs. Clients were going elsewhere to learn what EEI was teaching them, whether it was a Facebook group or a different online forum. EEI should have been in the middle of the growing online community, but it wasn't.

Options

EEI faced a major crossroads in 2009. No company can lose $240,000 in monthly revenue and continue to operate as if nothing happened. Changes were inevitable, but how they would manifest themselves remained unclear. Ultimately, EEI had to reorganize in an effort to make up the difference in lost revenue from the training business. That involved employee layoffs among other cost-cutting initiatives just to get the company back to breakeven.

At that point, EEI had two distinct choices in front of it: maintain the status quo or consider filing for bankruptcy. Admittedly, my knowledge of bankruptcy was minimal at the time, and the rest of EEI's executives weren't overly keen on exploring that option. Fighting through the economic downturn was viewed as the most reasonable choice.

Decision

By now you know the story: EEI eschewed bankruptcy in 2009 but ultimately ended up there in 2012. The decision not to file at the height of the recession bought the company three pressure-packed and stressful years of constant negotiation with landlords, bankers, and vendors, among others.

It's admirable to have faith that your business will succeed, but it's equally important to be able to step back and look clearly at the situation. EEI did not do an effective job of that. As a result, my job as CFO became heavily focused on workouts instead of helping the company invest in its future.

Outcome

Had EEI filed for bankruptcy in 2009, it would have saved time, energy, and money. EEI's business was bigger at that time than it was in 2012, and therefore had more revenue. That business revenue steadily diminished over the three-year period because, quite frankly, we were always playing catch-up.

If we made a profit, we weren't able to save it for reinvesting in the company's growth. We had to immediately spend it on a late rent payment, to an attorney, or to a vendor we owed money. Any excess cash flow we created wasn't used to grow the business because it was constantly used to plug the dam we had built instead.

If EEI had filed for bankruptcy in 2009 when things first took a negative turn, it could have had three years' worth of positive cash flow to build off. Instead, that money was used for paying down debt, settling with contractors, and extinguishing any other fires that arose. We spent a tremendous amount of money between 2009 and 2012 on things that weren't helping us for the future. It's frustrating in retrospect, but it serves as a valuable lesson.

Takeaways

One of the biggest advantages of bankruptcy is the built-in protection plan that comes with filing. From the moment your business files for bankruptcy until the moment it comes out, it's under bankruptcy protection.

We'll explore the bankruptcy protection period in greater detail later, but the gist is that other parties are prohibited from filing lawsuits, liens, or any other adverse action against your business while it's under protection. It simply can't be ignored how valuable this period of protection is to a business.

Not only does it instantly relieve the stress of having to deal with rising debts, but it also frees up time on your schedule so you can focus on the most important matter at hand: turning your business around. The bankruptcy protection period allows you to mute all of the noisy distractions that have been filling your ears so you can focus exclusively on your business. It's a major feeling of relief.

MAKE SMART CHOICES

EEI's decision to put off filing for bankruptcy for three years wasn't a smart decision. If bankruptcy can help your business, it's wise to file sooner rather than later. The earlier you do, the higher chance you will have of successfully turning around your business.

The future isn't as bleak as it might seem. Is your business thriving? If you felt the need to read this book, then it probably isn't right now. But can your business thrive in the future? Absolutely. Rather than focusing on the decisions and external factors that have led your business to this point, make prudent choices that can help it in the future.

We all stumble at times, but the key is to never stop moving forward. My triathlon training is excellent on some days and subpar on others. Sometimes I'm so energized after a strong run that I feel like I could finish first in the New York City Marathon. Other times I feel so tired and sore that I wonder if I can even finish the day's training. The reality is it's never as bad as you think, and it's usually never quite as good as you think either.

You should now have a much better understanding of when to file for bankruptcy than you did before you picked up this book, so use that knowledge to make a smart choice for your business. Stay on track. Don't get too high or too low. Bankruptcy is a triathlon race you can finish, but you have to maintain the right pace.

QUESTIONS TO CONSIDER

These questions at the end of each chapter are intended to help you evaluate your company. There are no right or wrong answers; every company's situation is unique. By answering the questions honestly, you'll get a better sense of whether your company could utilize bankruptcy as an effective tool.

- Are you currently being sued, or are you at risk to be sued in the future?
- Is the potential threat of your largest creditor significant?
- Has your business been operating at a break-even cash flow over the last sixty days?
- Is your company's value higher than its liquidation value?
- Do you have enough information to decide whether to file for bankruptcy?

Chapter Six

CHAPTER 11, NOW WHAT?

"Success is peace of mind, which is a direct result of self-satisfaction in knowing you made the effort to do your best to become the best that you are capable of becoming."

—JOHN WOODEN, LEGENDARY UCLA BASKETBALL COACH

When I emerge from the water after a 2.4-mile swim to start an IRONMAN triathlon, I feel like nothing can stop me. My adrenaline is pumping, my heart is racing, and every urge in my body is pushing me to race to my bike and take off peddling as fast as I possibly can. It's during that transition period between the swim and the 112-mile bike ride that I must remember to stay within my limits and respect my training.

I've been swimming for most of my life, and much of it at a high level, so it's reasonable for me to expect to finish the first IRONMAN stage in the top 10 percent. It's absolutely unreasonable for me to expect the same in the second and third stages. If I pushed myself too hard, too fast, I would be risking serious physical injury. My goal isn't to finish first—it's to finish. With that in mind, I consciously focus on my nutrition intake, my repetitions per minute, and my heart rate during races. If I just climbed a hill and my heart rate is above my target threshold, I'll back off.

That same mindset is needed when guiding your company through bankruptcy, which is a marathon, not a sprint. You have to trust those around you, including your legal counsel, as well as your own preparation. Take a step back and understand: Bankruptcy isn't a reflection of you. Your company isn't in bankruptcy because of something you did. Appreciate what you have in life. That simple yet powerful mindset helps me stay positive and motivated during the tough stretches of triathlon training and races, and it helped me keep bankruptcy in perspective.

WHY BANKRUPTCY IS SCARY

The early stages of bankruptcy are heavy on documentation. You will need lists of your vendors, creditors and associated debts, employees and the vacation time they've accrued, and updated payroll information. Your legal counsel will be better positioned to tell you exactly what is needed, but a general rule of thumb is to be overprepared rather than underprepared.

Bankruptcy will also draw your lending bank's attention. If you have a secured lender, you will need to agree on cash collateral agreement so that you can use the cash when client invoices are paid. The six-month window served as an additional motivation tool because you will need to show the bank you are making progress toward a plan. If the bank's senior credit committee feels you are not making a legitimate effort to turn around the business, they can decide to not renew the agreement, which would prohibit you from using any cash deposits for operations.

In the last chapter we reviewed the processes and procedures involved with the majority of successful Chapter 11 bankruptcy cases, but what about the unsuccessful cases? Not every business that files for bankruptcy will make it through. There are a variety of reasons why that might happen, but the possibility of an unknown outcome dissuades many business owners from seriously considering bankruptcy.

Many cases that begin in Chapter 11 don't reach the desired conclusion, instead ending in a controlled liquidation, sale, or auction. These options aren't ideal if you plan to continue to run the company for years to come, especially if you're using bankruptcy as a tool to reboot and reorient your business for long-term success. It's important to understand all of the possible outcomes:

- **Controlled liquidation:** If you begin to miss payments to creditors, your case can be forcefully converted to a Chapter 7 case. For instance, if a creditor doesn't receive a payment, they can file an official Chapter 7 conversion request with the court that states your company has failed to hold up its end of the judge-approved plan. If the request is granted, a trustee is appointed to oversee the liquidation of all assets and disbursement of any available cash.
- **Finding a buyer:** This is basically a Chapter 7 situation, but instead of being forced into liquidation by the court, you would find a buyer on your own. At that point, you could sell the assets of the business and use those proceeds to pay your creditors.
- **Equity auction:** One of the risks of going through Chapter 11 bankruptcy is that with all of the information on your company becoming public domain, it's possible another party could track everything and prepare a bid for your company without your knowledge.

STAYING ON TRACK

If someone wanted to start combing through bankruptcy filings to find a business they liked, monitor the case, and eventually place a bid in the equity auction, that is their right.

This type of public documentation is another turnoff to many business owners considering bankruptcy. That's certainly understandable. You get used to a nice, little private life as a business owner, but that goes away fairly quickly during bankruptcy. You have trustees, judges, creditors, and vendors, among many others, all asking you questions and digging into your finances. It's a vulnerable time that can leave you feeling exposed, almost as if you're living in a fishbowl.

Remember that bankruptcy can be a useful tool—one that's been used by countless business owners over the last few decades. You are not a failure to be ridiculed because bankruptcy is an option for your company. We can sometimes become our own worst enemy in situations that subject us to outside scrutiny, but remind yourself that other people are likely too busy with their own lives to care. Bankruptcy is a tried-and-true tool with a concise set of rules that allows you to operate your business without the distractions of legacy debts or the constant pressure to work out deals. The relief of those burdens alone makes dealing with the scrutiny of trustees, creditors, and the like better.

If you want to be able to focus on the future and improving your business instead of always running from the legacy debts and workouts, bankruptcy is a great option. If you have a business that can stand on its own but it's just inundated with problems from the past, bankruptcy will allow you to reorganize in a way that you can continue to move forward. The simple fact is the economy, customer behavior, and many other factors can change quicker than you are able to change your business, leaving you in a period that expenses far exceed revenue. Depending on the amount of cash you have saved and the length of time it takes you to respond, you might need a tool such as bankruptcy to address the debt that is created.

Bankruptcy is not a death sentence. It's an opportunity to reorganize in a meaningful way through a set of specific rules and a road map that guides you from point A to point B.

WHAT COMES NEXT

Point A in an IRONMAN triathlon is the entry point into the water for the swim, while point B is the finish line at the end of the 26.22-mile marathon. In between those two points is roughly fourteen hours of swimming, biking, running, and walking. There are no shortcuts. It's a long road with occasionally smooth stretches and difficult uphill climbs.

When I reach the second bike course loop, that's when I know I've hit the midway point of the race. That's also the hardest point because I'm already tired from the first half of the race and the sun beating down on me, yet I know I still have nearly ninety total miles still to go. Instead of focusing on the negativity, I choose to focus on other things that will help keep me in the moment: my nutrition, a song, counting, even daydreaming about a particularly encouraging training session. When I'm about to start the marathon, I don't think about the twenty-six miles to come. I focus on my first one hundred steps. After those one hundred steps, I set another short, attainable milestone and continue that for the entirety of the race.

Success, whether it's in an IRONMAN triathlon or running a business, is personal and unique to each individual. What qualifies as success to someone might be viewed as failure to another person. For the guy who is gunning to be a top-ten IRONMAN finisher, my goal of simply finishing is unacceptable. Only you know the goals for your business and how you define them. Follow the plan that can help you achieve those goals and avoid the distractions.

IRONMAN triathlons are by nature an individual challenge, but there is a sense of community in completing such a feat with hundreds and hundreds of other like-minded competitors. I soak up that shared feeling before and after the race, but during the race, I stay locked in on myself. For instance, one time while I was walking a stretch of the marathon, another competitor struck up a conversation with me. He was a perfectly pleasant guy and our chat was upbeat, even funny at times. But after a short while, I had to politely tell him I couldn't talk anymore. It had nothing to do with him personally, but if I continued to chitchat instead of focusing on my pacing, breathing, and hitting my target times, I would be doing myself a disservice. That's the same mindset to carry into bankruptcy.

CASE STUDY: THE FIRST HUNDRED DAYS

This chapter's installment focuses on the first three months after filing for bankruptcy and explains why it's a critical period.

Circumstances

The first hundred days after filing for bankruptcy are critical, regardless of the size of your business or the scope of your case. Those first three months were heavily focused on gathering pertinent data and attending meetings.

The biggest key at this stage is preparation. Bankruptcy was an entirely new experience for me, and it will be for you, too. Your best weapon is your own preparation, so come prepared.

Options

Our options during this period were somewhat limited by design. As you move forward through the bankruptcy process, the trustee and your legal counsel will lead the proceedings and maintain the schedule, but you've got to make sure you actively collect and manage any required information.

If you aren't on top of that, the trustee will take notice, and that's not ideal. Whether it's dealing with the trustee, creditors, or any other party, you want to keep them as happy as possible throughout the process. The better organized your company is from the start, the smoother your bankruptcy path will be.

Decision

As a CFO-turned-CEO, I've always taken great pride in keeping highly organized, accurate, and updated records. I've been fortunate to always have a passion for numbers, so it was never a challenge for me. If it is for you, make it a priority and find someone who can help you get organized.

During the first hundred days of bankruptcy, I did my best

impression of a sponge, soaking up every experience I could. I was mostly a spectator for the meetings with the trustee. I had made a conscious decision to learn as much about the process as I could, and there was no better hands-on experience.

Outcome

All told, I was in front of the judge only a handful of times during my bankruptcy process. Perhaps five times, but no more than six. This isn't unusual. The trustee is the person you will deal with more regularly.

After EEI's attorneys filed for bankruptcy, the next two steps were the 341 meeting, which is the initial introduction to the trustee assigned to your case, and the mailing of notices to all of your creditors.

The next meeting was held about a month later at the local courthouse. Myself, our CEO and EEI's counsel, the bank and its counsel, the landlord and their counsel, a handful of vendors, and the trustee were all present. It was an intimidating feeling. It almost felt like I was in trouble and had been called to the principal's office in school.

I was largely an observer, just trying to soak up as much information and knowledge about the process as possible. The attorneys representing each party do most of the talking, so there's a lot of legalese thrown around. It's a challenging experience, and I remember feeling frustrated and disappointed, sometimes at the same time.

Takeaways

I've been constantly stressing throughout this book how important it is to approach every step with a positive, optimistic mindset, and that sentiment still rings true now. However, it's not unusual to feel the sting of embarrassment at different points. Stay positive and focus on turning things around, not the missteps that led you to this point.

Also, the more you can get done behind the scenes before going in front of the judge, the better. Whether it's negotiating with creditors or accommodating the trustee in any way possible, do it. To trustees and judges, time is money, so don't waste it.

TRUST THE PROCESS

Often, bankruptcy can feel like a rigid, boring practice. There will be times that try your patience, but the process is structured for specific reasons. Trust it and be patient.

Are there days when the last thing I feel like doing is going for a long run? Of course. But I force myself to get up early and log the miles before work. Why? Because it's all part of the triathlon process.

If I skip one day of running, that enables my mind to convince itself that I can skip another day. And then another day and another. Before I know it, my entire training schedule is ruined. I'm only doing myself a disservice because it's going to come back to bite me hard on race day, if I'm even fit enough to compete.

There will be difficult days, but there will also be smooth ones. By staying the course and trusting the bankruptcy process, you will continue moving forward.

QUESTIONS TO CONSIDER

These questions at the end of each chapter are intended to help you evaluate your company. There are no right or wrong answers; every company's situation is unique. By answering the questions honestly, you'll get a better sense of whether your company could utilize bankruptcy as an effective tool.

- Is your company's financial accounting accurate and reliable?
- Are you comfortable with your company's finances becoming public record?
- Are your employee and vendor files organized and up to date?
- Is there someone on your team who can serve as a point of contact for vendor and employee questions?
- Are you mentally and emotionally prepared to face the bankruptcy process?

Chapter Seven

TURNING YOUR BUSINESS AROUND

———

"Have a plan. Follow the plan, and you'll be surprised how successful you can be. Most people don't have a plan. That's why it's easy to beat most folks."

—BEAR BRYANT, LEGENDARY
ALABAMA FOOTBALL COACH

As a race draws closer to its end, it's easy to become obsessed with the finish line. After a brutally long day swimming through rough waters, cycling over hot pavement, and alternately running and walking for 26 miles, all while baking under the sun's rays, sitting down in the shade with a cold drink sounds downright heavenly.

You might think that cool shade and delicious beverage

are the perfect motivation to finish the race on a strong note, but you have to resist the urge to push beyond your limits. The final stretch of the race is not the time to lose your discipline, which is the reason you've made it that far to begin with. Stay confident in yourself, trust your training, and block out everything that doesn't adhere to your plan.

Protecting yourself, your family, and your finances should always be part of your business plan, but one of the greatest benefits of bankruptcy is that it comes with a built-in protection period. From the day you file until the day you get out of bankruptcy, your business is under bankruptcy protection.

PROTECTION THROUGH BANKRUPTCY

The moment the court clerk stamps your case and enters it into the docket, bankruptcy protection begins. What does this mean, and why is it important? During the protection period, other parties are prevented from filing lawsuits against your company, putting liens against your business, or undertaking any other harmful motions. Vendors retain the right to end their working relationship with you at their own discretion. But if a vendor you owed money attempted to file suit against you, it would be rejected because that's something the bankruptcy process sorts out.

Bankruptcy is designed to give you the space you need to sort out where you are from a rearview-mirror perspective, develop a plan to move forward, and ultimately successfully execute that plan. The bankruptcy protection period puts a stop to any other parties' desire to put a lien against the business, put you into collections, get out of a contract, put you in default, and similar tactics so the plan can be effectively installed and implemented.

When creditors approach you regarding past due bills or threaten to file a lawsuit, you should respond with a short letter stating: *The company has filed for Chapter 11 bankruptcy. Here are the details. We're actively working on a plan. Submit your claim here by this date to be part of the plan. We appreciate your patience while the company works through this.*

This is a major benefit during the bankruptcy period as it entirely alleviates the potential headaches that others can inflict. Most people will understand and treat you fairly. If they've been around the business world long enough, they've likely already dealt with bankruptcy directly or indirectly.

The protection ends when the bankruptcy period ends, which can create a moment of panic as it opens the door for the old stresses to return. Unlike finishing an IRON-

MAN and thinking, "That wasn't so bad," the feeling is one of concern: Can we make this work? Can we live up to our plan? Will I be OK without the bankruptcy protection? The answer to all of those questions is the same: Yes.

STARTING THE TURNAROUND

After a lengthy bankruptcy process that can take multiple years, it can be a jarring adjustment to move out from under the protection period. If you haven't changed aspects of your business for the better, the possibility of falling back into old habits looms. Avoiding the same pitfalls that ultimately led your business to bankruptcy is necessary if you hope to achieve long-term stability and success.

Aside from adhering closely to the plan established during the bankruptcy process, your goal must be to run your business as if you were starting from scratch. That means operating with an intense, almost-exclusive focus on profitability. Most businesses are fundamentally sound at their core. What is the mission, the purpose of your business? Stripped of all the excess expenses and wasted time, what makes your business profitable? Carefully consider your answers to these questions.

Many businesses survive because the owner grinds away,

working endless hours for a net salary of $50,000 a year just to keep the wheels rolling. The reality is that type of commitment, workload, and responsibility should garner closer to $200,000 a year, so the business is actually losing $150,000. Some owners run their businesses for the lifestyle or as a hobby, so they're not overly concerned with the money they're pocketing at the end of the day. Analyzing the fundamental purpose of your business is one of the first steps in a successful turnaround strategy.

If you've gone through bankruptcy by this point, you're going to have tougher skin than you did when you first filed. My skin was certainly thicker by the time my company emerged from bankruptcy protection. It's not easy to be questioned on a weekly and monthly basis by banks, creditors, and judges, nor is it easy having your business's information available to the public. Dealing with clients, vendors, and your employees is easier, but it still tests your mettle at times. It's a challenging row to hoe, but it's all in the name of turning your business around. Positive change in the name of turnaround doesn't have to wait until your bankruptcy protection ends. In fact, it should start while you're under protection—and the sooner it starts, the better. You have only so much time and energy to dedicate to turning your business around. You're going to get there eventually, so you may as well get there quickly.

IDENTIFY AREAS OF CHANGE

EEI's biggest changes were in personnel and location. Our management team changed during the bankruptcy process, as did our location. Finding a new office space is challenging enough, but it's even trickier to find a landlord willing to take you on as a bankrupt company. In the end, we found a place. It was smaller and farther away from our old office, but it was reasonably priced and the landlord agreed to take us after a review of our financial situation.

Your company's areas of concern might be different, but it's important to review everything. Rent, leases, equipment, benefit packages—everything. The simplest and most effective way to do this is to evaluate your profit and loss statement. Find your highest expenses relative to your revenue and start there. Separate everything into one of two categories: must haves and hope to haves.

In fact, try running a scenario in which you put the first 10 percent of all cash received into an account you cannot access for one year. Then, run your business model on the resulting cash flow to identify which decisions you would need to make in order to survive. Once you've done that, try the same scenario with 25 percent and then 45 percent. Can you build a business model that is able to survive on 65 percent of all cash receipts, leaving the remaining 35 percent for profit, owner's compensation, and taxes?

When you're going to make a change, make it deeper than you're comfortable with. Don't be afraid to push yourself into new territory, and don't be afraid to make sacrifices when needed. Sure, it might be nice to have that expensive, deluxe copier that comes in handy every 180 days, but you'd save money by going to FedEx or a copy shop. It's convenient to have two people in the same position, but can the work they do be done effectively by just one person? You might be forced to answer these kinds of tough questions during a top-to-bottom, front-to-back evaluation of your business. Sometimes we become dependent on things we don't necessarily need. Bankruptcy offers the great opportunity to scrutinize your business. Find the fundamental reason you earn revenue and be aggressive.

CASE STUDY: GETTING OUT OF BANKRUPTCY

In the final installment of EEI's case study, we'll examine how the company got out of bankruptcy, as well as its steps for turning things around.

Circumstances

EEI filed for bankruptcy in early 2012 and was under protection until late 2014. At that point, EEI was officially out of bankruptcy, which is simultaneously a positive and negative feeling. It was positive because the company had made changes for the better and was coming off a strong year in 2014, but it was also negative because the safety net of bankruptcy protection was gone.

Once you're out of bankruptcy, you're still required to file quarterly reports for at least another year. Those are mostly a formality to ensure you are following the plan set forth during bankruptcy. EEI was doing just that.

Options

When EEI came out of bankruptcy, I was the CEO and new owner of the company. I went from referring to it as "a company" to "our company," which took some getting used to. My mentality post-bankruptcy was simple: focus on what we're great at.

EEI's biggest strength at the time was its publishing and editing services. We had a handful of staffing contracts that brought in money, and we had a pair of recruiters who managed those contracts. The cash flow process was solid: offer a professional editing or publishing service, bill the client, get paid. Rinse, repeat. As long as we managed that process effectively, we could keep the cash flow even.

That was the easy part. The trickier part was dealing with the pesky training business, the same branch of the company that had taken a financial beating back in 2009. Something had to be done.

Decision

The training business came with considerable expense and overhead. For each course offered through EEI, an office or conference room had to be rented. Equipment had to rented and set up. Computers had to be flushed to remove any of the previous day's content. On top of that, the cash flow process was different than the editorial business: the majority of payments came in before the class ran, as opposed to billing after the fact.

Added together, it was a major headache and resource drain for the branch of the company that desperately needed an infusion of technology. I knew it needed an upgrade, and I didn't even have to read the constant negative reviews on Yelp to know that (although I did read some and they weren't good for business).

I had made the decision to finally address EEI's training business in a permanent way, but I still wasn't sure how that would take shape. After I connected with a local venture capital accelerator, a plan began to take shape.

Outcome

Typically, venture capital accelerators offer money in exchange for equity in a company. After I met with a handful of the partners in this specific accelerator group, we reached an interesting idea: What if we could find a CEO who would run the training business for equity? That way, we could spin the training business out of EEI completely, allowing the company to focus solely on what it did best.

One of the reasons 2014 was such a strong year for EEI was that the company focused on only its professional services. The training business was moderately successful in this new model for about a year and half before it puttered out. I had hoped the accelerator group would fall in love with it within six months and then invest more money to push the online angle, but it never happened. The training business fizzled away, but EEI's core editing service remained strong.

Takeaways

When EEI came out of bankruptcy, the payment plan was reasonable. We had to pay court fees, but our bank payments were manageable.

According to the model, our growth rate and size would allow it to absorb its monthly payment without much notice. Of course, that growth rate had accounted for the training business still bringing in money, but we were having a solid year in 2014. We made all scheduled payments on time, made all of our rent payments, paid all of our employees, and took care of our vendors.

By the time the calendar turned to 2015, EEI was facing another issue. Hiccups will pop up every now and then in every business, no matter how stable or successful. That's just the nature of the beast, and it's another reason to have a nest egg or line of credit. But when we lost two revenue-driving staffing contracts, I had to figure out a way to get EEI back to profitability. Just as I had done with the training business, I closed down EEI's staffing business. What had once been a three-pronged company offering editorial, staffing, and training services was now exclusively an editorial services company. This brings us back to the point of focusing on what you're great at, what makes the phone ring. For EEI, that was its editorial services.

By the end of 2016, our editorial business was humming. We were making a little bit of a profit after having reduced so much of our expenses and overhead. By 2016, we had a small staff with small real estate and technology requirements. At the end of the day, I saw EEI as a great niche business for people who needed perfect content.

KEEP THE END IN MIND

When you emerge from bankruptcy, the main task on your plate is executing the plan devised during bankruptcy.

That's simple, in theory, but without the official protection the bankruptcy period provides, distractions have a way of popping up.

How can you combat distractions and remain dialed in on the plan? Have an end goal in mind. I knew I wanted to streamline EEI by reducing its expenses and focusing squarely on its true strength, but I couldn't do that in one day.

Stick to your plan by focusing your attention on daily tasks. Over time, smaller goals like making rent payments on time will build until you're able to meet your larger business goals.

QUESTIONS TO CONSIDER

These questions at the end of each chapter are intended to help you evaluate your company. There are no right or wrong answers; every company's situation is unique. By answering the questions honestly, you'll get a better sense of whether your company could utilize bankruptcy as an effective tool.

- Have you developed a plan to make your business profitable tomorrow?
- Do you understand what your business is investing in?

- Can your business successfully achieve its thirteen-week cash flow forecast?
- Do you trust your financial officer or manager?
- Are you prepared to face bankruptcy head-on?

CONCLUSION

TRUST YOURSELF

———

Bankruptcy has forever changed me. When I think back to the sleepless nights spent scouring the Internet for any sliver of advice, I'm floored by how far I've come. All I wanted was a guide that not only explained the ins and outs of the bankruptcy process but also offered guidance on a deeper emotional and psychological level. The knowledge gained from my own personal experience with EEI is the reason this book exists, and it's the book I wish I had at my disposal when the company I worked for faced bankruptcy.

Getting through bankruptcy has opened my eyes to possibilities I never previously considered as a business owner. Whereas I initially feared EEI would lose all of its clients and vendors by filing for bankruptcy, I came to understand the opposite was true. Bankruptcy doesn't put you out of business. In fact, it can make you a stronger business. Clients and vendors are people, too, and they want to work. If you're able to service them or they're able to help you service your clients, that's going to matter more than your company being in bankruptcy.

Like most people with only a cursory knowledge of bankruptcy, I thought initially it was a death sentence for EEI and a permanent scarlet letter for myself. It was neither. The bankruptcy process is a tool, not a noose. Many companies go through it, and most have successful outcomes. Yes, it's an expensive and time-consuming process, but when you compare it to the opportunity to reduce debts systematically and turn around your company, it's a smart investment. Bankruptcy offers a chance to restart, and that's a worthwhile venture. Always remember: Bankruptcy is not failure, and you are not in this alone.

KEEP THINGS IN PERSPECTIVE

When I was younger, I loved to sit at the windowsills of my parents' house. It was dangerous, sure, but there were screens in the windows and I was young, invincible, and in love with the views. One summer day when I was four years old, I was sitting in one of the windowsills enjoying the refreshing breeze. It was just a perfect day—not too hot, with a light wind that caressed my skin. I was, of course, perched in the most comfortable spot in the house, but on that particular day, I got a bit too comfortable. I feel asleep sitting in the windowsill and woke up in the hospital.

I had fallen asleep in the windowsill, leaning against the screen. After a few minutes, the screen gave way to the pressure and I tumbled ten-plus feet to the ground below. My father was out in the backyard cutting wood with a chainsaw for the wood stove, so it was my mother who found me lying unconscious on the ground, bleeding from ears, nose, and mouth. My parents rushed me to the hospital, and aside from some bumps and bruises, it turned out I was fine.

I think about this story from time to time to remind myself how fortunate I am. What's fortunate about falling out a window, you ask? My parents' house had a large concrete slab for a front porch, no more than four inches from where my head landed. Had I been in a different window-sill or merely moved my body in a slightly different way, I could have died that day at four years old. I'm lucky to be alive and I'm lucky to be able to do the things that I do. I carry that mentality throughout life, whether it's running a business, finishing an IRONMAN triathlon, playing with my kids, or just having a cold beer. I've had times where I found myself in negative spirals, but by keeping a happy, healthy, and appreciative perspective on life, I've always been able to overcome them.

YOU CONTROL YOUR DESTINY

There's a fine line between trying to make the most of your life and believing your purpose is predetermined. If you believed your life was set for you, what's the incentive to try new things? I'm a firm believer that certain people are meant to walk specific paths in life, but you still have to work hard for everything you get.

I'm not big on zodiac signs, although I admit I'll check the horoscope for cancers out of curiosity if I'm flipping through the *Wall Street Journal* or *Washington Post*. I place much more stock in astrology charts, and I have my mother to thank for that. She compiled my astrology chart when I was still an infant, and as mentioned earlier in the book, the results were amazingly accurate. The chart indicated I was destined not only to work with numbers but also to face down challenging paths when others shied away from them. I'd say my journey with EEI—from CFO of a successful company to CEO of one in bankruptcy—fits that bill.

Life will never stop throwing you curveballs, but how

you react to them reveals who you are. When my parents discovered my older brother Paul was handicapped, they were devastated. If you are a parent, recall the indescribable joy you felt when you first held your child. It's one of the most cherished memories in my life. For my parents, however, that moment was the same happiness and joy mixed with horror, anger, and sadness. Their devastation over my brother's handicap could have led to a series of lawsuits, attorney fees, and other legal entanglements. But that wasn't the future my mother wanted for Paul. She eventually asked my father, "Why are we spending all of this negative energy on the hospital when we should be focusing on Paul and what's positive?" I'm still blown away by her strength to think like that, and it's inspired me to always find the positives in life.

When compared to life-and-death situations, bankruptcy suddenly seems far less threatening. If I could get through it with no prior knowledge or experience, there's no doubt you can when armed with the lessons gleaned from this book.

Let's quickly review what we've covered in the previous seven chapters:

- What bankruptcy is and isn't.
- How the three most prominent forms are classified.

- How to assess your financial picture.
- Who to turn to for advice and guidance.
- If and when you should file.
- What information needs to be prepared.
- How to strategize an exit plan.

If you are fully aware of these seven key facts, you will be ready to effectively use bankruptcy as a tool to put your business on a new path forward.

BANKRUPTCY IS A TRIATHLON

The bankruptcy process can be confusing, uninviting, and downright scary. By studying the ins and outs and preparing for different outcomes, you will alleviate those feelings. It's not going to be cheap or easy, but many of the most rewarding things in life aren't either. On a personal level, completing two IRONMAN triathlons—with more to come in the future—is a major achievement. On a professional level, guiding EEI through bankruptcy is a major achievement. Both required months of preparation and training, and both were challenging in their own ways.

Positive things happen to positive people. That's not a cliché—I truly believe it to be true. I've carried that mentality throughout my life, and it's enabled me to achieve these milestones. By utilizing bankruptcy as a helpful tool, you'll be able to effectively hit the reset button and take control of your business for the better.

No one can cross the finish line of an IRONMAN triathlon without these four traits: toughness, intelligence, preparation, and commitment. Those same traits apply to every business owner who has successfully navigated bankruptcy. I recently read a quote that really hit home for me: "Entrepreneurship is living a few years of your life like most people won't, so that you can spend the rest of your life like most people can't." I can't even begin to count the number of times over my years with EEI that people have asked me, "Why are you doing this?" It's hard to explain why I'm committed to something that, in so many others' views, wasn't worth the time, effort, and energy. I felt a great sense of pride and ownership, so I stuck with EEI instead of leaving to become a financial analyst or CFO somewhere else.

Do I hope that one day I have the finer things in life that other people dream of? Absolutely. I want to go skydiving, travel the world, send my children to the best schools, and all of the other things that seem like luck to others. The difference is, I understand those things won't come from luck or a predetermined fate in life. They'll come from the hard work and dedication I've put in during my decade at EEI. To make that kind of life a reality, I'm willing to do what others won't.

I'm lucky to be where I am in life and to have accomplished the things I have. I take time every day to appreciate and be grateful for what I have, my family and my health chief among them. It's absolutely imperative that you do the same as you face bankruptcy. Don't settle for breakeven anymore. Break the rut your business has fallen into and take action to fix the situation. You'll be happier in the long term, and bankruptcy is an effective tool to help you achieve that.

French psychologist Émile Coué once famously said, "Every day, in every way, I'm getting better and better." Never forget that you are, too.

APPENDIX

SELECTED ACTIONS DURING BANKRUPTCY CASE

First Week after Filing

- Chapter 11 Voluntary Petition, Verification of Creditor Matrix, Statement of Financial Affairs
- Support Document—Corporate Resolution
- Notice of Meeting of Creditors. Meeting to be held in 30 days. Proof of Claim due 120 days after creditor meeting.
- 20 Largest Unsecured Creditors
- Equity Security Holders
- Application to Employ Law Firm and Verified Statement of Proposed Party
- Emergency Motion to Shorten Time
- Emergency Motion to Pay Pre-Petition Wages
- Support Document—20 largest unsecured creditors

- Emergency Motion to Use Cash Collateral
- Notice of Hearing related to Use Cash Collateral

First Month after Filing

- Hearing Held regarding Use Cash Collateral
- Consent Order Approving First Interim Agreement for Use of Cash Collateral
- Application to Employ Accounting Firm to File Annual Tax Returns
- Motion to Reject Nonresidential Lease
- Motion for Continuation of Utility Service
- US Trustee's Meeting of Creditors Report

First Six Months after Filing

- Monthly Operating Report (ongoing monthly until confirmation)
- Consent Motion Approving Second Interim Agreement for Use of Cash Collateral
- Consent Order Approving Second Interim Agreement for Use of Cash Collateral
- Order Enlarging Exclusivity Period to File Plan
- Motion to Reject Equipment Leases

First Year after Filing

- Chapter 11 Plan of Reorganization Filed
- Disclosure Statement Filed
- Amended Chapter 11 Plan of Reorganization
- Objection on behalf of US Trustee
- Objection on behalf of Senior Creditor

Remaining Time

- Order Denying Approval of Plan and Granting 90 Days to Amend
- Amended Chapter 11 Plan and Disclosure Statement
- Order Fixing Deadline to File Administrative Claims
- Order Approving Bidding Procedures in Connection with the Sale of Equity Interests
- Tally of Ballots
- Order Confirming Plan
- Hearing Held Auction to Solicit Higher and Best for the Equity Interests
- Order Approving Bidder of Equity Interest
- Post-Confirmation Quarterly Operating Report
- Chapter 11 Final Report, Account, and Application
- Final Decree and Close Bankruptcy Case

LIQUIDATION ANALYSIS

CHAPTER 7 | LIQUIDATION ANALYSIS–EDITORIAL EXPERTS, INC.

ASSETS	BOOK VALUE	LIQUIDATION VALUE
Cash	$10,000	$10,000
Accounts Receivable	$514,963	$257,481
Real Property	N/A	N/A
Personal Property	$77,165	$16,500
Total Assets	$602,128	$283,981
LIABILITIES Secured Debt		($598,500)
Chapter 7 Administration		($10,326)
Administrative Expenses of Case		($170,000)
Unsecured Nonpriority Creditors		($882,003)
Total Liabilities		($1,660,829)

AMOUNTS AVAILABLE IN CHAPTER 7 FOR UNSECURED DEBT: $0

CASH FLOW ANALYSIS (EXAMPLE)

PAYMENT DATE	NAME	PAYMENT AMOUNT	DUE DATE	AGING
5-Jan-07	Rent	$2,000	21-Nov-06	45
12-Jan-07	Vendor A	$500	29-Oct-06	75
17-Jan-07	Payroll	$5,000	17-Jan-07	0
19-Jan-07	Vendor B	$1,000	25-Mar-06	300
26-Jan-07	Vendor C	$750	26-Jan-07	0
27-Jan-07	Payroll	$5,000	27-Jan-07	0
27-Jan-07	Vendor D	$4,000	27-Jan-06	365
31-Jan-07	Vendor E	$8,000	25-Jul-06	190

CASH FLOW ANALYSIS (CONT.)

PAYMENT ANALYSIS				BALANCE REMAINING	PAYMENT/ PAST DUE
CURRENT	60 DAYS	180 DAYS	180+ DAYS		
	$2,000			$7,000	22.2%
		$500		–	100%
$5,000				–	100%
			$1,000	$3,000	25%
$750				$750	50%
$5,000				–	100%
			$4,000	$4,000	50%
			$8,000	$10,000	44%
$10,750	$2,000	$500	$13,000	$24,750	

	CURRENT	60 DAYS	180 DAYS	180+ DAYS
% OF ALL PAYMENTS:	41%	7.6%	1.9%	49.5%
% OF NON PAYROLL PAYMENTS:	4.6%	12.3%	3.1%	80%

ANALYSIS: This company spent a majority of it non-payroll cash flow on aged vendors who continued to have significant balances after the payments. This situation will most likely lead to further issues as new bills age. Company should consider dramatic changes in order to shore up cash flow.

13-WEEK CASH FLOW MODEL (PARTIAL)

WEEK# WEEK BEGINNING MONDAY	WEEK 1 9/23/2011	WEEK 2 9/30/2011	WEEK 3 10/7/2011	WEEK 4 10/14/2011	WEEK 5 10/21/2011
RECEIPTS					
Collections from P/S/CT AR	90,000	90,000	90,000	90,000	90,000
Receipts from Open Training	20,000	20,000	20,000	20,000	20,000
Miscellaneous Income	–	–	–	–	–
TOTAL RECEIPTS	110,000	110,000	110,000	110,000	110,000
PAYROLL DISBURSEMENTS					
Salary and Wages and Taxes	–	95,000	–	95,000	–
Payroll Liabilities	45,000	–	45,000	–	45,000
Other					
TOTAL PAYROLL RELATED	45,000	95,000	45,000	95,000	45,000
GENERAL DISBURSEMENTS					
Existing AP	50,000	15,000	50,000	15,000	50,000
Other	–	–	–	–	–
TOTAL GEN. DISBURSEMENTS	50,000	15,000	50,000	15,000	50,000
TOTAL GEN. DISBURSEMENTS AND PAYROLL RELATED	95,000	110,000	95,000	110,000	95,000
OPERATING NET CASH FLOW	15,000	–	15,000	–	15,000
OTHER DISBURSEMENTS > EQUITY, NEW DEBT > DEBT PAYMENTS (OTHER)					
Interest	–	–	–	–	–
Principal Payments	–	–	–	–	–
TOTAL OTHER DISBURSEMENTS	–	–	–	–	–
TOTAL DISBURSEMENTS	95,000	110,000	95,000	110,000	95,000
TOTAL NET CASH FLOW	15,000	–	15,000	–	15,000
ROLL FORWARD TOTAL NET CASH FLOW	155,810	155,810	170,810	170,810	185,810

ABOUT THE AUTHOR

——

GREGORY K. MCDONOUGH is a seasoned executive who creates energizing solutions to difficult business situations. He has owned and operated businesses in the professional services industry, and he mentors companies ranging from start-ups to $100 million enterprises. As a Certified Insolvency and Restructuring Advisor, he has led companies through turnarounds, mergers, acquisitions, and other financial matters. McDonough is involved with the Entrepreneurs's Organization, Association for Corporate Growth, and the British-American Business Association. A veteran of multiple Ironman Triathlons, he publishes blogs with his wife on triathlon training as well as on parenting.

www.ingramcontent.com/pod-product-compliance
Lightning Source LLC
Chambersburg PA
CBHW071556200326
41519CB00021BB/6781